St. Louis
Walk *of* Fame

140 Great St. Louisans

What an inspiring city!

Joe Edwards

St. Louis Walk of Fame
140 Great St. Louisans

ISBN: 978-0-9821386-1-8

GENERAL INFORMATION

write or email
St. Louis Walk of Fame
6504 Delmar Blvd.
St. Louis, MO 63130
info@stlouiswalkoffame.org

ORDERING INFORMATION

Individual Orders
Order online at stlouiswalkoffame.org or send
$25.00 plus $7.95 shipping and handling to
St. Louis Walk of Fame
6504 Delmar Blvd.
St. Louis, MO 63130

Schools and Businesses
For information about quantity discounts with bulk purchases for educational, business, gift, sales or promotional purposes, write to the address above or email info@stlouiswalkoffame.org

All proceeds received from the sale of this book go directly to the nonprofit St. Louis Walk of Fame.

Visit the St. Louis Walk of Fame website at stlouiswalkoffame.org

Printed in the United States of America

St. Louis
Walk *of* Fame

140 Great St. Louisans

with a foreword by founder Joe Edwards

Table of Contents

St. Louis Walk of Fame *140 Great St. Louisans*

Foreword

The St. Louis Walk of Fame is a nonprofit organization founded in 1988 to provide a showcase for the cultural heritage of St. Louis and to advance the knowledge, awareness and appreciation of great St. Louisans and their accomplishments. Its mission is also to encourage pride in the community and career inspiration in individuals.

The Walk of Fame consists of brass stars and bronze plaques embedded in the sidewalks of the Delmar Loop to honor people from the St. Louis area who have made major national contributions to our cultural heritage. Each star features the name of an honoree and the accompanying plaque contains a biography summarizing his or her achievements and connection to the city. These informative plaques distinguish the St. Louis Walk of Fame from similar projects throughout the country and make ours educational as well as entertaining.

The St. Louis Walk of Fame highly values education and donates copies of its book to the libraries of all St. Louis metropolitan area junior high schools and high schools where they are used for school projects, research projects and reading for plain enjoyment. One will frequently see school field trips in The Loop making chalk rubbings of the plaques on paper for their projects.

The Walk provides examples of role models from all walks of life and areas of achievement – everyone can identify with somebody on it who stirs motivation in them.

Please enjoy this book and come visit the St. Louis Walk of Fame – it's free, open all year round and easily accessible. I hope that it gives you knowledge, inspiration and great pleasure.

Joe Edwards
Founder

Nomination Criteria

Nominees for the St. Louis Walk of Fame must fulfill two main criteria:

1   They must have been born in St. Louis or have spent their formative or creative years here.

2   Their accomplishments must have had a national impact on our cultural heritage.

Many accomplished St. Louisans qualify for one but not the other condition. Perhaps he or she did not reside in the St. Louis area long enough to be firmly associated with the city or did not spend formative or creative years here. Perhaps due to the nature of the person's work, his or her contributions and achievements did not have a national impact, even though the impact locally was immense.

Nomination Process

There are approximately 250 great St. Louisans from the past and present on the list of nominees. They represent national luminaries from fields such as art, music, architecture, literature, journalism, civil rights, education, science, political activism, sports, acting, entertainment and broadcasting.

Anyone may participate in the nomination process. Simply send a letter to the St. Louis Walk of Fame office with the name, date and place of birth and a short history of the person you wish to nominate. Include the person's St. Louis connection and a description of his or her national impact.

Nominations Committee
St. Louis Walk of Fame
6504 Delmar in The Loop
St. Louis, MO 63130-4501

Selection Process

120 St. Louisans are on the Walk of Fame selection committee. The committee includes the chancellors of all area universities; key people from local libraries, arts organizations and historical societies; media journalists; and other citizens with an informed understanding of St. Louis' cultural heritage.

The selection committee is 51% female and 49% male; it is 71% white, 27% African-American and 2% Asian-American. Ballots are mailed to selection committee members in the summer of each year and the new inductees are announced the following spring.

Induction Ceremonies

The St. Louis Walk of Fame's induction ceremonies are lively, entertaining and frequently moving. A live band plays ragtime and Dixieland jazz, setting the celebratory mood. Presenters and accepting inductees delight the crowd with their words which have been spoken in all sorts of styles. Comedienne Phyllis Diller and baseball great Yogi Berra each had the audience doubled over in laughter. Olympic athlete Jackie Joyner-Kersee and author and professor Gerald Early gave profound, stirring speeches. Jazz musician Clark Terry pulled out his fluegelhorn and began playing.

Inductees have said that being inducted into their hometown's Walk of Fame is a particularly special honor to receive in their careers. Whether the ceremonies are larger like those from 1989 through 2004 with five to ten inductees and a keynote speaker, or whether they're more intimate like the ceremonies since then that honor and focus on one inductee, St. Louis' culture and history are celebrated and everyone is invited.

Joe Edwards, founder

1992 ceremony

St. Louis River Critters Band

Chuck Berry, 1989

Stan Musial, 1993

Yogi Berra, Gyo Obata, Joe Garagiola and Shelley Winters, 1992

Nelly, 2010

John Goodman, 1997

John Goodman

Leonard Slatkin, Howard Nemerov,
William Danforth and Willie Mae Ford Smith, 1990

William Gass, Red Schoendiest and
Johnnie Johnson, 1998

St. Louis Walk of Fame *140 Great St. Louisans*

Jackie Joyner-Kersee, 2000

Phyllis Diller, 1993

Lou Brock and A.E. Hotchner, 1994

William Danforth, Harriett Woods, Dick Weber and John Hartford, 1999

Clark Terry, 1996

ceremony in 2011

Max Starkloff, 2008

Cedric the Entertainer, 2008

Jackie Joyner-Kersee, Robert Guillaume and Fontella Bass, 2000

Maya Angelou and Grace Bumbry one month prior to ceremony, 1992

St. Louis Walk of Fame *140 Great St. Louisans*

Bill McClellan, 1997

Ray Hartman, 1999

Harriett Woods, 1989

Keynote Speakers

1989	Harriett Woods women's activist and Missouri Lt. Governor
1990	William Danforth Chancellor, Washington University
1991	William Woo Editor, *St. Louis Post-Dispatch*
1992	Gwen Stephenson Chancellor, St. Louis Community College
1993	Stan Musial baseball Hall of Famer and Cardinals great
1994	Greg Freeman columnist, *St. Louis Post-Dispatch*
1995	Blanche Touhill Chancellor, University of Missouri-St. Louis
1996	Clarence Harmon Chief of Police and Mayor of St. Louis
1997	Bill McClellan columnist, *St. Louis Post-Dispatch*
1998	Karen Foss news anchor, KSDK-TV
1999	Ray Hartmann Editor, *Riverfront Times*
2000	Robert Guillaume star of television, theater and film
2001	Nan Wyatt KMOX radio journalist
2002	Julius Hunter author and KMOV-TV news anchor
2003	Jill McGuire Executive Director of the Regional Arts Commission
2004	Dr. Henry Givens President of Harris-Stowe State College

Location

The St. Louis Walk of Fame's brass stars and informative plaques are set in the sidewalks along the 6100–6600 blocks of Delmar Boulevard in the vibrant Delmar Loop, designated "One of the 10 Great Streets in America" by the American Planning Association. Centrally located in the St. Louis metropolitan area, The Loop offers a rich cultural experience while one browses the St. Louis Walk of Fame, with over 140 specialty shops including restaurants, galleries, unique gift stores, music and book stores, clothing boutiques, live music spaces and performing arts venues.

The Loop is easily accessible from four major highways and from the Delmar Loop MetroLink station. Ample parking, including for tour and school buses, is available throughout this historic district making this unique, free Walk available to all for enjoyment and education.

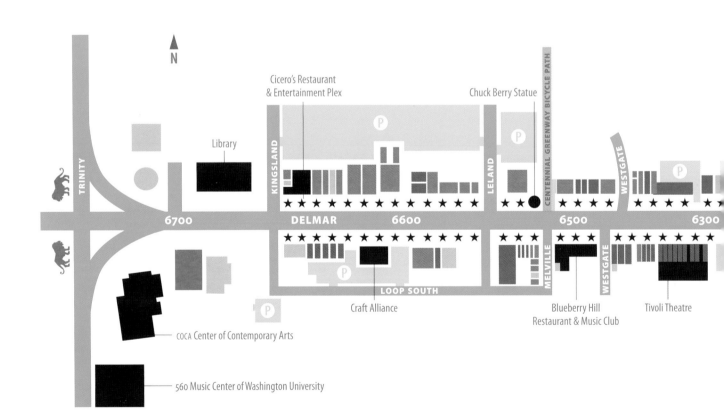

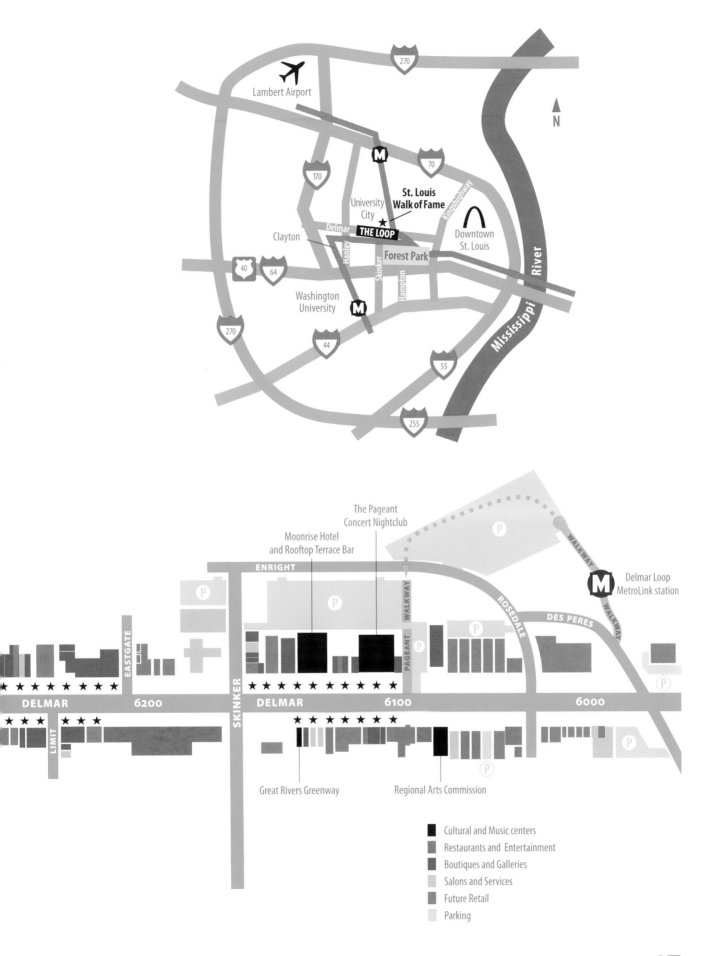

Lambert Airport

270

170

70

M

St. Louis
Walk of Fame

University
City

Delmar   THE LOOP

Clayton

Forest Park

Downtown
St. Louis

Hanley

Skinker

Hampton

King'sHighway

40

64

Washington
University

M

270

44

55

Mississippi River

255

N

The Pageant
Concert Nightclub

Moonrise Hotel
and Rooftop Terrace Bar

P

ENRIGHT

WALKWAY

P

P

WALKWAY

Delmar Loop
MetroLink station

M

EASTGATE

P

ROSEDALE

DES PERES

SKINKER

PAGEANT

★ ★ ★ ★ ★ ★ ★ ★ ★

DELMAR   6200

DELMAR   6100

6000

P

★ ★ ★ ★ ★   ★ ★ ★

LIMIT

★ ★ ★ ★ ★ ★ ★ ★

P

P

Great Rivers Greenway

Regional Arts Commission

■ Cultural and Music centers
■ Restaurants and Entertainment
■ Boutiques and Galleries
■ Salons and Services
■ Future Retail
■ Parking

List of Inductees by Field of Achievement

 Acting & Entertainment

Josephine Baker
Scott Bakula
Cedric the Entertainer
Phyllis Diller
Katherine Dunham
Robert Duvall
Buddy Ebsen
Redd Foxx
John Goodman
Betty Grable
Dick Gregory
Charles Guggenheim
Robert Guillaume
William Holden
Kevin Kline
Rocco Landesman
Marsha Mason
Virgina Mayo
David Merrick
Agnes Moorehead
Vincent Price
Harold Ramis
The Rockettes
Mary Wickes
Shelley Winters

 **Art & Architecture**

James B. Eads
Charles Eames
Mary Engelbreit
Walker Evans
Al Hirschfeld
William Ittner
Theodore Link
Gyo Obata
Charles M. Russell
Ernest Trova
Chic Young

 Broadcasting

Jack Buck
Harry Caray
Bob Costas
Joe Garagiola
Dave Garroway

⭐ **General Category**

Disability Rights Activism
Max Starkloff

Statesman
David Francis

Aviation
Charles A. Lindbergh

City Founder
Auguste Chouteau
Pierre Laclède

Civil Rights
Dred and Harriet Scott

Explorer
William Clark

Military
William T. Sherman

Military & U.S. President
Ulysses S. Grant

Politics & Activism
William "Bill" Clay
John Danforth
Tom Eagleton
Harriett Woods

 Journalism

Elijah Lovejoy
Bill Mauldin
Mike Peters
Joseph Pulitzer

Literature

Maya Angelou
William Burroughs
Kate Chopin
Gerald Early
T.S. Eliot
Stanley Elkin
Eugene Field
William Gass
Martha Gellhorn
A.E. Hotchner
William Inge
Marrianne Moore
Howard Nemerov
Irma Rombauer
Ntozake Shange
Sara Teasdale
Kay Thompson
Mona Van Duyn
Tennessee Williams

 Music

Fontella Bass
Mel Bay
Chuck Berry
Grace Bumbry
Miles Davis
5th Dimension
John Hartford
Donny Hathaway
Johnnie Johnson
Scott Joplin
Albert King
Michael McDonald
Robert McFerrin, Sr.
Nelly
David Sanborn
Leonard Slatkin
Willie Mae Ford Smith
Clark Terry
Henry Townsend
Helen Traubel
Ike Turner
Tina Turner

 Science & Education

Susan Blow
Robert S. Brookings
Barry Commoner
Arthur Holly Compton
Carl and Gerty Cori
William Danforth
William Greenleaf Eliot
Evarts Graham
Masters and Johnson
Marlin Perkins
Peter Raven
Paul C. Reinert, S.J.
Henry Shaw

 Sports

Henry Armstrong
Cool Papa Bell
Yogi Berra
Lou Brock
Jimmy Connors
Dwight Davis
Dizzy Dean
Dan Dierdorf
Curt Flood
Bob Gibson
Whitey Herzog
Rogers Hornsby
Hale Irwin
Jackie Joyner-Kersee
Ed Macauley
Archie Moore
Stan Musial
Bob Pettit
Judy Rankin
Branch Rickey
Red Schoendienst
George Sisler
Jackie Smith
Ozzie Smith
Dick Weber

List of Inductees
by Year of Birth

	Month/Day of Birth	Year of Birth	Month/Day of Death	Year of Death
Pierre Laclède	11/22	1729	6/20	1778
Auguste Chouteau	9/7	1749	2/24	1829
William Clark	8/1	1770	9/1	1838
Dred Scott	unknown	c. 1799	9/17	1858
Henry Shaw	7/24	1800	8/25	1889
Elijah Lovejoy	11/9	1802	11/7	1837
William Greenleaf Eliot	8/5	1811	1/23	1887
Harriet Scott	unknown	c. 1820	6/17	1876
William T. Sherman	2/8	1820	2/14	1891
James B. Eads	5/23	1820	3/8	1887
Ulysses S. Grant	4/27	1822	7/23	1885
Susan Blow	6/7	1843	3/26	1916
Joseph Pulitzer	4/10	1847	10/29	1911
Robert S. Brookings	1/22	1850	11/15	1932
Theodore Link	3/17	1850	11/12	1923
Eugene Field	9/2	1850	11/4	1895
David Francis	10/1	1850	1/15	1927
Kate Chopin	2/8	1851	8/22	1904
Charles M. Russell	3/19	1864	10/24	1926
William Ittner	9/4	1864	1/26	1936
Scott Joplin	11/24	1868	4/1	1917
Irma Rombauer	10/30	1877	10/14	1962
Dwight Davis	7/5	1879	11/28	1945
Branch Rickey	12/20	1881	12/9	1965
Evarts Graham	3/19	1883	3/4	1957
Sara Teasdale	8/8	1884	1/29	1933
Marrianne Moore	11/15	1887	2/5	1972
T.S. Eliot	9/26	1888	1/4	1965
Arthur Holly Compton	9/10	1892	3/15	1962
George Sisler	3/24	1893	3/26	1973
Rogers Hornsby	4/27	1896	1/5	1963

	Month/Day of Birth	Year of Birth	Month/Day of Death	Year of Death
Gerty Cori	8/15	1896	10/26	1957
Carl Cori	12/5	1896	10/20	1984
Helen Traubel	6/16	1899	7/28	1972
Agnes Moorehead	12/6	1900	4/30	1974
Chic Young	1/9	1901	3/14	1973
Charles A. Lindbergh	2/4	1902	8/26	1974
Marlin Perkins	3/28	1902	6/14	1986
Cool Papa Bell	5/17	1903	3/7	1991
Al Hirschfeld	6/21	1903	1/20	2003
Walker Evans	11/3	1903	4/10	1975
Willie Mae Ford Smith	6/23	1904	2/2	1994
Josephine Baker	6/3	1906	4/12	1975
Charles Eames	6/17	1907	8/21	1978
Buddy Ebsen	4/2	1908	7/6	2003
Martha Gellhorn	11/8	1908	2/15	1998
Katherine Dunham	6/22	1909	5/21	2006
Henry Townsend	10/27	1909	9/24	2006
Kay Thompson	11/9	1909	7/2	1998
Dizzy Dean	1/16	1910	7/17	1974
Mary Wickes	6/13	1910	10/22	1995
Paul C. Reinert, S.J.	8/12	1910	7/22	2001
Tennessee Williams	3/26	1911	2/25	1983
Vincent Price	5/27	1911	10/25	1993
David Merrick	11/27	1911	4/25	2000
Henry Armstrong	12/12	1912	10/22	1988
Mel Bay	2/25	1913	5/14	1997
William Inge	5/3	1913	6/10	1973
Dave Garroway	7/13	1913	7/21	1982
Archie Moore	12/13	1913	12/9	1998
William Burroughs	2/5	1914	8/2	1997
Harry Caray	3/1	1914	2/18	1998
William Masters	12/27	1915	2/16	2001
Betty Grable	12/18	1916	7/2	1973
Barry Commoner	5/28	1917	9/30	2012
Phyllis Diller	7/17	1917	8/20	2012
William Holden	4/17	1918	11/12	1981
Howard Nemerov	3/1	1920	7/5	1991

	Month/Day of Birth	Year of Birth	Month/Day of Death	Year of Death
A.E. Hotchner	6/28	1920		
Shelley Winters	8/18	1920	1/14	2006
Stan Musial	11/21	1920	1/19	2013
Virgina Mayo	11/30	1920	1/17	2005
Clark Terry	12/14	1920		
Robert McFerrin, Sr.	3/19	1921	11/24	2006
Mona Van Duyn	5/9	1921	12/2	2004
Bill Mauldin	10/29	1921	1/22	2003
Redd Foxx	12/9	1922	11/11	1991
Red Schoendienst	2/2	1923		
Gyo Obata	2/28	1923		
Albert King	4/25	1923	12/21	1992
Charles Guggenheim	3/31	1924	10/9	2002
Johnnie Johnson	7/8	1924	4/13	2005
William Gass	7/30	1924		
Jack Buck	8/21	1924	6/18	2002
Virginia Johnson	2/11	1925	7/24	2013
Yogi Berra	5/12	1925		
The Rockettes		1925		
Joe Garagiola	2/12	1926		
William Danforth	4/10	1926		
Miles Davis	5/26	1926	9/28	1991
Chuck Berry	10/18	1926		
Ernest Trova	2/19	1927	3/8	2009
Harriett Woods	6/2	1927	2/8	2007
Robert Guillaume	11/30	1927		
Ed Macauley	3/22	1928	11/8	2011
Maya Angelou	4/4	1928		
Tom Eagleton	9/4	1929	3/4	2007
Dick Weber	12/23	1929	2/14	2005
Stanley Elkin	5/11	1930	5/31	1995
Robert Duvall	1/5	1931		
William "Bill" Clay	4/30	1931		
IkeTurner	11/5	1931	12/12	2007

	Month/Day of Birth	Year of Birth	Month/Day of Death	Year of Death
Whitey Herzog	11/9	1931		
Dick Gregory	10/12	1932		
Bob Pettit	12/12	1932		
Bob Gibson	11/9	1935		
Peter Raven	6/13	1936		
John Danforth	9/5	1936		
Grace Bumbry	1/4	1937		
Max Starkloff	9/18	1937	12/27	2010
John Hartford	12/30	1937	6/4	2001
Curt Flood	1/18	1938	1/20	1997
Lou Brock	6/18	1939		
Tina Turner	11/26	1939		
Jackie Smith	2/23	1940		
Fontella Bass	7/3	1940	12/26	2012
Marsha Mason	4/3	1942		
Mike Peters	10/9	1943		
Leonard Slatkin	9/1	1944		
Harold Ramis	11/21	1944		
Judy Rankin	2/18	1945		
Hale Irwin	6/3	1945		
David Sanborn	7/30	1945		
Donny Hathaway	10/1	1945	1/13	1979
Rocco Landesman	7/20	1947		
Kevin Kline	10/24	1947		
Ntozake Shange	10/18	1948		
Dan Dierdorf	6/29	1949		
Michael McDonald	2/12	1952		
Bob Costas	3/22	1952		
Gerald Early	4/21	1952		
Mary Engelbreit	6/5	1952		
John Goodman	6/20	1952		
Jimmy Connors	9/2	1952		
Scott Bakula	10/9	1954		
Ozzie Smith	12/26	1954		
Jackie Joyner-Kersee	3/3	1962		
Cedric the Entertainer	4/24	1964		
5th Dimension		1965		
Nelly	11/2	1974		

List of Inductees
by Month and Day of Birth

	Month/Day of Birth	Year of Birth		Month/Day of Birth	Year of Birth
Grace Bumbry	1/4	1937	Buddy Ebsen	4/2	1908
Robert Duvall	1/5	1931	Marsha Mason	4/3	1942
Dizzy Dean	1/16	1910	Maya Angelou	4/4	1928
Curt Flood	1/18	1938	Joseph Pulitzer	4/10	1847
Chic Young	1/9	1901	William Danforth	4/10	1926
Robert S. Brookings	1/22	1850	William Holden	4/17	1918
Red Schoendienst	2/2	1923	Gerald Early	4/21	1952
Charles A. Lindbergh	2/4	1902	Cedric the Entertainer	4/24	1964
William Burroughs	2/5	1914	Albert King	4/25	1923
William T. Sherman	2/8	1820	Ulysses S. Grant	4/27	1822
Kate Chopin	2/8	1851	Rogers Hornsby	4/27	1896
Virginia Johnson	2/11	1925	William "Bill" Clay	4/30	1931
Joe Garagiola	2/12	1926	William Inge	5/3	1913
Michael McDonald	2/12	1952	Mona Van Duyn	5/9	1921
Judy Rankin	2/18	1945	Stanley Elkin	5/11	1930
Ernest Trova	2/19	1927	Yogi Berra	5/12	1925
Jackie Smith	2/23	1940	Cool Papa Bell	5/17	1903
Mel Bay	2/25	1913	James B. Eads	5/23	1820
Gyo Obata	2/28	1923	Miles Davis	5/26	1926
Harry Caray	3/1	1914	Vincent Price	5/27	1911
Howard Nemerov	3/1	1920	Barry Commoner	5/28	1917
Jackie Joyner-Kersee	3/3	1962	Harriett Woods	6/2	1927
Theodore Link	3/17	1850	Josephine Baker	6/3	1906
Charles M. Russell	3/19	1864	Hale Irwin	6/3	1945
Evarts Graham	3/19	1883	Mary Engelbreit	6/5	1952
Robert McFerrin, Sr.	3/19	1921	Susan Blow	6/7	1843
Ed Macauley	3/22	1928	Mary Wickes	6/13	1910
Bob Costas	3/22	1952	Peter Raven	6/13	1936
George Sisler	3/24	1893	Helen Traubel	6/16	1899
Tennessee Williams	3/26	1911	Charles Eames	6/17	1907
Marlin Perkins	3/28	1902	Lou Brock	6/18	1939
Charles Guggenheim	3/31	1924	John Goodman	6/20	1952

	Month/Day of Birth	Year of Birth		Month/Day of Birth	Year of Birth
Al Hirschfeld	6/21	1903	Kevin Kline	10/24	1947
Katherine Dunham	6/22	1909	Henry Townsend	10/27	1909
Willie Mae Ford Smith	6/23	1904	Bill Mauldin	10/29	1921
A.E. Hotchner	6/28	1920	Irma Rombauer	10/30	1877
Dan Dierdorf	6/29	1949	Nelly	11/2	1974
Fontella Bass	7/3	1940	Walker Evans	11/3	1903
Dwight Davis	7/5	1879	Ike Turner	11/5	1931
Johnnie Johnson	7/8	1924	Martha Gellhorn	11/8	1908
Dave Garroway	7/13	1913	Elijah Lovejoy	11/9	1802
Phyllis Diller	7/17	1917	Kay Thompson	11/9	1909
Rocco Landesman	7/20	1947	Whitey Herzog	11/9	1931
Henry Shaw	7/24	1800	Bob Gibson	11/9	1935
William Gass	7/30	1924	Marrianne Moore	11/15	1887
David Sanborn	7/30	1945	Stan Musial	11/21	1920
William Clark	8/1	1770	Harold Ramis	11/21	1944
William Greenleaf Eliot	8/5	1811	Pierre Laclède	11/22	1729
Sara Teasdale	8/8	1884	Scott Joplin	11/24	1868
Paul C. Reinert, S.J.	8/12	1910	Tina Turner	11/26	1939
Gerty Cori	8/15	1896	David Merrick	11/27	1911
Shelley Winters	8/18	1920	Virgina Mayo	11/30	1920
Jack Buck	8/21	1924	Robert Guillaume	11/30	1927
Leonard Slatkin	9/1	1944	Carl Cori	12/5	1896
Eugene Field	9/2	1850	Agnes Moorehead	12/6	1900
Jimmy Connors	9/2	1952	Redd Foxx	12/9	1922
William Ittner	9/4	1864	Henry Armstrong	12/12	1912
Tom Eagleton	9/4	1929	Bob Pettit	12/12	1932
John Danforth	9/5	1936	Archie Moore	12/13	1913
Auguste Chouteau	9/7	1749	Clark Terry	12/14	1920
Arthur Holly Compton	9/10	1892	Betty Grable	12/18	1916
Max Starkloff	9/18	1937	Branch Rickey	12/20	1881
T.S. Eliot	9/26	1888	Dick Weber	12/23	1929
David Francis	10/1	1850	Ozzie Smith	12/26	1954
Donny Hathaway	10/1	1945	William Masters	12/27	1915
Mike Peters	10/9	1943	John Hartford	12/30	1937
Scott Bakula	10/9	1954	Dred Scott	unknown	c. 1799
Dick Gregory	10/12	1932	Harriet Scott	unknown	c. 1820
Chuck Berry	10/18	1926	The Rockettes		1925
Ntozake Shange	10/18	1948	5th Dimension		1965

Location of Stars
by Inductee Name

All addresses are on Delmar in The Loop

Maya Angelou	6337	Dan Dierdorf	6642
Henry Armstrong	6622	Phyllis Diller	6366
Josephine Baker	6501	Katherine Dunham	6513
Scott Bakula	6148	Robert Duvall	6195
Fontella Bass	6691	James B. Eads	6635
Mel Bay	6178	Tom Eagleton	6633
Cool Papa Bell	6265	Charles Eames	6606
Yogi Berra	6322	Gerald Early	6263
Chuck Berry	6504	Buddy Ebsen	6303
Susan Blow	6374	T.S. Eliot	6191
Lou Brock	6602	William Greenleaf Eliot	6676
Robert S. Brookings	6197	Stanley Elkin	6275
Jack Buck	6307	Mary Engelbreit	6679
Grace Bumbry	6319	Walker Evans	6695
William Burroughs	6362	Eugene Field	6315
Harry Caray	6321	5th Dimension	6164
Cedric the Entertainer	6166	Curt Flood	6162
Kate Chopin	6310	Redd Foxx	6331
Auguste Chouteau	6358	David Francis	6669
William Clark	6619	Joe Garagiola	6328
William "Bill" Clay	6267	Dave Garroway	6627
Barry Commoner	6342	William Gass	6632
Arthur Holly Compton	6329	Martha Gellhorn	6665
Jimmy Connors	6681	Bob Gibson	6352
Carl and Gerty Cori	6605	John Goodman	6508
Bob Costas	6502	Betty Grable	6350
John Danforth	6308	Evarts Graham	6305
William Danforth	6638	Ulysses S. Grant	6394
Dwight Davis	6621	Dick Gregory	6611
Miles Davis	6314	Charles Guggenheim	6636
Dizzy Dean	6643	Robert Guillaume	6640

John Hartford	6638	Vincent Price	6509
Donny Hathaway	6156	Joseph Pulitzer	6515
Whitey Herzog	6152	Harold Ramis	6338
Al Hirschfeld	6301	Judy Rankin	6146
William Holden	6150	Peter Raven	6605
Rogers Hornsby	6699	Paul C. Reinert, S.J.	6650
A.E. Hotchner	6608	Branch Rickey	6631
William Inge	6624	The Rockettes	6309
Hale Irwin	6176	Irma Rombauer	6636
William Ittner	6661	Charles M. Russell	6388
Johnnie Johnson	6628	David Sanborn	6306
Scott Joplin	6510	Red Schoendienst	6634
Jackie Joyner-Kersee	6683	Dred and Harriet Scott	6647
Albert King	6370	Ntozake Shange	6160
Kevin Kline	6630	Henry Shaw	6346
Pierre Laclède	6317	William T. Sherman	6685
Rocco Landesman	6128	George Sisler	6651
Charles A. Lindbergh	6519	Leonard Slatkin	6318
Theodore Link	6617	Jackie Smith	6655
Elijah Lovejoy	6332	Ozzie Smith	6664
Ed Macauley	6672	Willie Mae Ford Smith	6392
Marsha Mason	6646	Max Starkloff	6170
Masters and Johnson	6380	Sara Teasdale	6187
Bill Mauldin	6271	Clark Terry	6623
Virgina Mayo	6620	Kay Thompson	6660
Michael McDonald	6668	Henry Townsend	6610
Robert McFerrin, Sr.	6300	Helen Traubel	6193
David Merrick	6677	Ernest Trova	6335
Archie Moore	6648	Ike Turner	6659
Marrianne Moore	6625	Tina Turner	6378
Agnes Moorehead	6604	Mona Van Duyn	6273
Stan Musial	6502	Dick Weber	6636
Nelly	6508	Mary Wickes	6304
Howard Nemerov	6500	Tennessee Williams	6500
Gyo Obata	6325	Shelley Winters	6323
Marlin Perkins	6505	Harriett Woods	6640
Mike Peters	6644	Chic Young	6174
Bob Pettit	6272		

Location of Stars
by Street Number

All addresses are on Delmar in The Loop

6128	Rocco Landesman		6306	David Sanborn
6146	Judy Rankin		6307	Jack Buck
6148	Scott Bakula		6308	John Danforth
6150	William Holden		6309	The Rockettes
6152	Whitey Herzog		6310	Kate Chopin
6156	Donny Hathaway		6314	Miles Davis
6160	Ntozake Shange		6315	Eugene Field
6162	Curt Flood		6317	Pierre Laclède
6164	5th Dimension		6318	Leonard Slatkin
6166	Cedric the Entertainer		6319	Grace Bumbry
6170	Max Starkloff		6321	Harry Caray
6174	Chic Young		6322	Yogi Berra
6176	Hale Irwin		6323	Shelley Winters
6178	Mel Bay		6325	Gyo Obata
6187	Sara Teasdale		6328	Joe Garagiola
6191	T.S. Eliot		6329	Arthur Holly Compton
6193	Helen Traubel		6331	Redd Foxx
6195	Robert Duvall		6332	Elijah Lovejoy
6197	Robert S. Brookings		6335	Ernest Trova
6263	Gerald Early		6337	Maya Angelou
6265	Cool Papa Bell		6338	Harold Ramis
6267	William "Bill" Clay		6342	Barry Commoner
6271	Bill Mauldin		6346	Henry Shaw
6272	Bob Pettit		6350	Betty Grable
6273	Mona Van Duyn		6352	Bob Gibson
6275	Stanley Elkin		6358	Auguste Chouteau
6300	Robert McFerrin, Sr.		6630	Kevin Kline
6301	Al Hirschfeld		6362	William Burroughs
6303	Buddy Ebsen		6366	Phyllis Diller
6304	Mary Wickes		6370	Albert King
6305	Evarts Graham		6374	Susan Blow

6378	Tina Turner	6632	William Gass
6380	Masters and Johnson	6633	Tom Eagleton
6388	Charles M. Russell	6634	Red Schoendienst
6392	Willie Mae Ford Smith	6635	James B. Eads
6394	Ulysses S. Grant	6636	Charles Guggenheim
6500	Howard Nemerov	6636	Irma Rombauer
6500	Tennessee Williams	6636	Dick Weber
6501	Josephine Baker	6638	William Danforth
6502	Bob Costas	6638	John Hartford
6502	Stan Musial	6640	Robert Guillaume
6504	Chuck Berry	6640	Harriett Woods
6505	Marlin Perkins	6642	Dan Dierdorf
6508	John Goodman	6643	Dizzy Dean
6508	Nelly	6644	Mike Peters
6509	Vincent Price	6646	Marsha Mason
6510	Scott Joplin	6647	Dred and Harriet Scott
6513	Katherine Dunham	6648	Archie Moore
6515	Joseph Pulitzer	6650	Paul C. Reinert, S.J.
6519	Charles A. Lindbergh	6651	George Sisler
6602	Lou Brock	6655	Jackie Smith
6604	Agnes Moorehead	6659	Ike Turner
6605	Carl and Gerty Cori	6660	Kay Thompson
6605	Peter Raven	6661	William Ittner
6606	Charles Eames	6664	Ozzie Smith
6608	A.E. Hotchner	6665	Martha Gellhorn
6610	Henry Townsend	6668	Michael McDonald
6611	Dick Gregory	6669	David Francis
6617	Theodore Link	6672	Ed Macauley
6619	William Clark	6676	William Greenleaf Eliot
6620	Virgina Mayo	6677	David Merrick
6621	Dwight Davis	6679	Mary Engelbreit
6622	Henry Armstrong	6681	Jimmy Connors
6623	Clark Terry	6683	Jackie Joyner-Kersee
6624	William Inge	6685	William T. Sherman
6625	Marrianne Moore	6691	Fontella Bass
6627	Dave Garroway	6695	Walker Evans
6628	Johnnie Johnson	6699	Rogers Hornsby
6631	Branch Rickey		

Dates of Ceremonies
with Acceptors

	Field of Achievement	Date of Ceremony	Acceptor
Maya Angelou	*Literature*	5/17/1992	Eugene B. Redmond, Poet Laureate of East St. Louis
Henry Armstrong	*Sports*	5/21/1995	Edna Nashville, stepdaughter
Josephine Baker	*Acting & Entertainment*	5/20/1990	Richard Martin, nephew
Scott Bakula	*Acting & Entertainment*		
Fontella Bass	*Music*	5/21/2000	self
Mel Bay	*Music*	6/30/2011	William Bay, son, and Susan Bay Banks, daughter
Cool Papa Bell	*Sports*	5/19/1991	Connie Brooks, daughter
Yogi Berra	*Sports*	5/17/1992	self
Chuck Berry	*Music*	6/25/1989	self
Susan Blow	*Science & Education*	5/19/1991	Carolyn George, President of the Susan E. Blow Foundation
Lou Brock	*Sports*	5/15/1994	self
Robert S. Brookings	*Science & Education*	6/23/2011	Dr. William Danforth, former Washington University Chancellor
Jack Buck	*Broadcasting*	5/19/1991	Carole Buck, wife
Grace Bumbry	*Music*	5/17/1992	Benjamin Bumbry, Jr., brother
William Burroughs	*Literature*	5/20/1990	Kenn Thomas, Thomas Jefferson Library, UMSL
Harry Caray	*Broadcasting*	5/16/1993	Dutchie Caray, wife
Cedric the Entertainer	*Acting & Entertainment*	6/7/2008	self
Kate Chopin	*Literature*	5/20/1990	George Chopin, grandson
Auguste Chouteau	*General Category City Founder*	5/16/1993	Peter Michel, Missouri Historical Society
William Clark	*General Category Explorer*	5/19/1996	Carolyn Gilman, Missouri Historical Society
William "Bill" Clay	*General Category Politics & Activism*	10/2/2006	self

	Field of Achievement	Date of Ceremony	Acceptor
Barry Commoner	*Science & Education*	5/16/1993	self
Arthur Holly Compton	*Science & Education*	5/17/1992	Clifford Will, Professor and Chairman of Physics, Washington University
Jimmy Connors	*Sports*	5/20/2001	Bill Lelly, friend
Carl and Gerty Cori	*Science & Education*	5/15/1994	Dr. Gary Ackers, Washington University School of Medicine, Biochemistry and Molecular Biophysics
Bob Costas	*Broadcasting*	5/21/1995	Pam Reichman, business manager and personal assistant
John Danforth	*General Category Politics & Activism*	5/16/2004	self
William Danforth	*Science & Education*	5/16/1999	self
Dwight Davis	*Sports*	5/19/1996	Tom O'Neal, Founder, St. Louis Tennis Hall of Fame
Miles Davis	*Music*	5/20/1990	Charlie Rose, jazz musician
Dizzy Dean	*Sports*	5/18/1997	Bob Forsch, baseball Cardinal pitching great
Dan Dierdorf	*Sports*	5/19/2002	self
Phyllis Diller	*Acting & Entertainment*	5/16/1993	self
Katherine Dunham	*Acting & Entertainment*	6/25/1989	Bonita Cornute, KTVI-TV
Robert Duvall	*Acting & Entertainment*		
James B. Eads	*Art & Architecture*	6/25/1989	Howard Miller, History Department, UMSL
Tom Eagleton	*General Category Politics & Activism*	5/18/1997	self
Charles Eames	*Art & Architecture*	5/15/1994	Carl Safe, Washington University School of Architecture
Gerald Early	*Literature*	4/11/2013	self
Buddy Ebsen	*Acting & Entertainment*	5/19/1991	Steve Cox, author, *Beverly Hillbillies*
T.S. Eliot	*Literature*	6/25/1989	Leslie Konnyu, Founder, T.S. Eliot Society
William Greenleaf Eliot	*Science & Education*	5/11/2003	Dr. Mark Wrighton, Chancellor, Washington University
Stanley Elkin	*Literature*	5/19/1991	self

Dates of Ceremonies
with Acceptors, cont.

	Field of Achievement	Date of Ceremony	Acceptor
Mary Engelbreit	*Art & Architecture*	5/20/2001	self
Walker Evans	*Art & Architecture*	5/21/2000	Michael Eastman, photographer
Eugene Field	*Literature*	5/19/1991	John Scholz, Director, Eugene Field House and Toy Museum
5th Dimension	*Music*	3/18/2010	Billy Davis, Jr. and Lamonte McLemore, 5th Dimension founding members
Curt Flood	*Sports*		
Redd Foxx	*Acting & Entertainment*	5/17/1992	Lavell Crawford, comedian
David Francis	*General Category Statesman*		
Joe Garagiola	*Broadcasting*	5/17/1992	self
Dave Garroway	*Broadcasting*	5/19/1996	Paris Garroway Neurock, daughter
William Gass	*Literature*	5/17/1998	self
Martha Gellhorn	*Literature*		
Bob Gibson	*Sports*	5/16/1993	Stan Musial, baseball Cardinal Hall of Famer
John Goodman	*Acting & Entertainment*	5/18/1997	self
Betty Grable	*Acting & Entertainment*	5/20/1990	Audrey Birk, childhood friend
Evarts Graham	*Science & Education*		
Ulysses S. Grant	*General Category Military & U.S. President*	5/20/1990	Jerry Schober, National Park Service for White Haven, Grant's Home
Dick Gregory	*Acting & Entertainment*	5/21/1995	self
Charles Guggenheim	*Acting & Entertainment*	10/29/2005	Marion Guggenheim, wife, and Grace Guggenheim, daughter
Robert Guillaume	*Acting & Entertainment*	5/16/1999	Pat Carpenter, daughter
John Hartford	*Music*	5/16/1999	self
Donny Hathaway	*Music*		
Whitey Herzog	*Sports*		
Al Hirschfeld	*Art & Architecture*	5/16/1993	Joe Edwards, St. Louis Walk of Fame

	Field of Achievement	Date of Ceremony	Acceptor
William Holden	*Acting & Entertainment*	8/9/2012	Brian Keller, President of the O'Fallon Historical Society
Rogers Hornsby	*Sports*	5/21/2000	Fred Hanser, St. Louis Cardinals Chairman
A.E. Hotchner	*Literature*	5/15/1994	self
William Inge	*Literature*	5/21/1995	Henry Schvey, Chairman, Performing Arts Department, Washingon University
Hale Irwin	*Sports*		
William Ittner	*Art & Architecture*	10/4/2008	Reed Ittner Voorhees, great-grandson
Johnnie Johnson	*Music*	5/17/1998	self
Scott Joplin	*Music*	6/25/1989	Annette Bridges, site administrator, Scott Joplin House
Jackie Joyner-Kersee	*Sports*	5/21/2000	self
Albert King	*Music*	5/16/1993	Chuck Berry, Rock and Roll Hall of Famer
Kevin Kline	*Acting & Entertainment*	5/17/1998	Joe Edwards, St. Louis Walk of Fame
Pierre Laclède	*General Category City Founder*	5/16/1993	Kathy Corbett, Missouri Historical Society
Rocco Landesman	*Acting & Entertainment*	6/11/2013	self
Charles A. Lindbergh	*General Category Aviation*	6/25/1989	Judy Little, President, University City Historical Society
Theodore Link	*Art & Architecture*	5/21/1995	Carolyn Toft, Executive Director, Landmarks Association
Elijah Lovejoy	*Journalism*	5/17/1992	Reverend Robert Tabscott, President, Elijah Lovejoy Society
Ed Macauley	*Sports*	5/11/2003	self
Marsha Mason	*Acting & Entertainment*	5/19/2002	Marita Woodruff, Marsha Mason's drama instructor at Webster College
Masters and Johnson	*Science & Education*	5/19/1991	selves
Bill Mauldin	*Journalism*	5/19/1991	Martin Quigley, author
Virgina Mayo	*Acting & Entertainment*	5/19/1996	self
Michael McDonald	*Music*	5/11/2003	Kathy Walker, sister
Robert McFerrin, Sr.	*Music*	5/16/2004	self
David Merrick	*Acting & Entertainment*	5/20/2001	Judith Newmark, theater critic, *St. Louis Post-Dispatch*

Dates of Ceremonies
with Acceptors, cont.

	Field of Achievement	Date of Ceremony	Acceptor
Archie Moore	*Sports*	5/19/2002	Evelyn O. Rice-Peebles, Commissioner of Recreation, City of St. Louis
Marrianne Moore	*Literature*	5/19/1996	Professor Dan Shea, Chairman, English Department, Washington University
Agnes Moorehead	*Acting & Entertainment*	5/15/1994	Carrie Houk, St. Louis Film Partnership
Stan Musial	*Sports*	6/25/1989	Joe Edwards, St. Louis Walk of Fame
Nelly	*Music*	10/15/2010	self
Howard Nemerov	*Literature*	5/20/1990	self
Gyo Obata	*Art & Architecture*	5/17/1992	self
Marlin Perkins	*Science & Education*	5/20/1990	Carol Perkins, wife
Mike Peters	*Journalism*	5/19/2002	self
Bob Pettit	*Sports*	5/14/2009	self
Vincent Price	*Acting & Entertainment*	6/25/1989	Barbara Gay, niece
Joseph Pulitzer	*Journalism*	6/25/1989	William F. Woo, Editor, *St. Louis Post-Dispatch*
Harold Ramis	*Acting & Entertainment*	5/16/2004	Henry Schvey, Chairman, Performing Arts Department, Washingon University
Judy Rankin	*Sports*	4/29/2013	self
Peter Raven	*Science & Education*	5/21/1995	self
Paul C. Reinert, S.J.	*Science & Education*	5/19/2002	Father Lawrence Biondi, S.J., President, St. Louis University
Branch Rickey	*Sports*	5/18/1997	Stephen S. Adams III, grandson
The Rockettes	*Acting & Entertainment*	8/1/2007	Karilyn Ashley Surratt and Lara Turek, current Rockettes
Irma Rombauer	*Literature*	5/17/1998	Jeff Rombauer, grandson
Charles M. Russell	*Art & Architecture*	5/19/1991	Will Fulkerson, relative
David Sanborn	*Music*	5/16/2004	Sallie Sanborn, sister
Red Schoendienst	*Sports*	5/17/1998	self
Dred and Harriet Scott	*General Category Civil Rights*	5/18/1997	Kathryn Nelson, educator and activist, and Stephanie Gathright, great-great-granddaughter

	Field of Achievement	Date of Ceremony	Acceptor
Ntozake Shange	*Literature*	9/14/2012	self
Henry Shaw	*Science & Education*	5/16/1993	Dr. Peter Raven, Director, Missouri Botanical Garden
William T. Sherman	*General Category Military*	5/21/2000	U.S. Army Major General Robert Flowers
George Sisler	*Sports*	10/22/2005	Dave Sisler, son, and Frances Drochelman, daughter
Leonard Slatkin	*Music*	5/20/1990	self
Jackie Smith	*Sports*	5/20/2001	self
Ozzie Smith	*Sports*	5/11/2003	self
Willie Mae Ford Smith	*Music*	5/20/1990	self
Max Starkloff	*General Category Disability Rights Activism*	6/20/2008	self
Sara Teasdale	*Literature*	5/15/1994	Dr. David Hadas, English Department, Washington University
Clark Terry	*Music*	5/19/1996	self
Kay Thompson	*Literature*	5/11/2003	Ms. Lorin Cuoco, author and NPR Reporter
Henry Townsend	*Music*	5/21/1995	self
Helen Traubel	*Music*	5/15/1994	Charles Mackay, Managing Director, Opera Theater of St. Louis
Ernest Trova	*Art & Architecture*	5/17/1992	Adam Aronson, art collector and patron
Ike Turner	*Music*	5/20/2001	self
Tina Turner	*Music*	5/19/1991	Oliver Sain, St. Louis rhythm & blues great
Mona Van Duyn	*Literature*	5/16/1993	self
Dick Weber	*Sports*	5/16/1999	self
Mary Wickes	*Acting & Entertainment*	5/16/2004	Dennis Reagan, President and CEO of The Muny
Tennessee Williams	*Literature*	6/25/1989	Dakin Williams, brother
Shelley Winters	*Acting & Entertainment*	5/17/1992	self
Harriett Woods	*General Category Politics*	5/16/1999	self
Chic Young	*Art & Architecture*		

Maya Angelou

BORN APRIL 4, 1928

Maya Angelou, born Marguerite Johnson in St. Louis,
was raised in segregated rural Arkansas. Her best-selling
account of that upbringing, *I Know Why the Caged Bird
Sings*, won critical acclaim in 1970. A leading literary
voice of the African-American community, Angelou
wrote a dozen more books of prose and poetry, earning
Pulitzer Prize and National Book Award nominations.
She was also nominated for an Emmy Award for her
acting in *Roots*, and her screenplay *Georgia, Georgia*
was the first by a black woman to be filmed. An eminent
lecturer, Maya Angelou became a professor of American
Studies at Wake Forest University in 1981.

37

Henry Armstrong

BORN DECEMBER 12, 1912

The only boxer to hold world titles in three weight classes simultaneously, Henry Armstrong moved to St. Louis as a young boy and was an honor student at Vashon High School. Known as "Perpetual Motion," he dominated feather, welter and lightweight opponents with his "blackout" punch, relentless attack and incredible stamina. After 152 victories in 14 years, Armstrong retired in 1945. Returning to St. Louis, he became a minister, helped run the Herbert Hoover Boys' Club and trained young boxers. One of the first inductees when the Boxing Hall of Fame opened in 1954, Henry Armstrong is considered one of the top three boxers of all time.

Josephine Baker

BORN JUNE 3, 1906

As a child in St. Louis, Josephine Baker rummaged for
coal behind Union Station and for food behind Soulard
Market. At age 13 she waitressed at the Chauffeurs' Club
on Pine Street and danced with a minstrel band. In 1925
she went to Paris with the Revue Nègre. She starred in the
Folies Bergère the next season and became one of France's
best-loved entertainers. During World War II, she was a
heroine of the Resistance, earning the Légion d'Honneur.
A French citizen, she was an activist for civil rights in
the United States. On her death in 1975, she was given
an unprecedented state funeral in Paris.

Scott Bakula

BORN OCTOBER 9, 1954

Actor Scott Bakula was born in St. Louis and graduated from Kirkwood High in 1973. His first success came in the theatre, both on and off Broadway, and he was nominated for a Tony in 1988. Bakula became a household name as Dr. Sam Beckett on *Quantum Leap*, the 1989–1993 television series that inspired an ardent following. Bakula later starred in *Star Trek: Enterprise* from 2001 to 2005, and returned to television in 2009 in *Men of a Certain Age*. Bakula's many films include *Lord of Illusions* (1995), *Cats Don't Dance* (1997), *American Beauty* (1999) and *The Informant!* (2009). A star of stage, film and television, Scott Bakula is among the most recognizable actors of his generation.

Fontella Bass

BORN JULY 3, 1940

Fontella Bass, daughter of gospel great Martha Bass, was born and raised in St. Louis. She played piano and sang with R&B stars Little Milton and Oliver Sain, and launched her solo career in 1965 with the electrifying "Rescue Me," a #1 R&B and #4 pop hit. After three years performing in Paris with Lester Bowie and the Art Ensemble of Chicago, she returned to St. Louis in 1972 to raise her family. Always sharing her musical gift in local churches, she went on to perform internationally and at Carnegie Hall. 1995's Grammy-nominated album *No Ways Tired* and 1999's *Speaking in Tongues* showcase the extraordinary talents of Fontella Bass.

Mel Bay

BORN FEBRUARY 25, 1913

Mel Bay bought his first guitar at age thirteen, taught himself to play and was performing publicly within a few months. He moved to St. Louis in 1933, where he fronted his own trio and taught up to 100 students per week. In 1947 Bay published his landmark instruction manual *The Orchestral Chord System for Guitar*, soon followed by *Modern Guitar Method*. Marvels of simple yet thorough instruction, Bay's various guitar manuals sold over 25 million copies. Called "the George Washington of the guitar" by Guitar Player magazine, Mel Bay promoted guitar popularity worldwide by making the instrument easily accessible to novice players while helping expert musicians improve their technique.

Cool Papa Bell

BORN MAY 17, 1903

Major league baseball was closed to blacks until 1947, relegating some of the game's best players to the Negro Leagues. One of them was James Thomas Bell, who joined the St. Louis Stars in 1922. Nicknamed Cool Papa for his composure, Bell played and coached professional baseball for 29 years. Known as the fastest player ever, Cool Papa often stole two bases on one pitch or scored from second on a sacrifice fly. Satchel Paige said Bell could turn off the light and "be in bed before the room was dark." He batted .400 several times and stole 175 bases in one year. Cool Papa Bell was inducted into the Baseball Hall of Fame in 1974.

Yogi Berra

BORN MAY 12, 1925

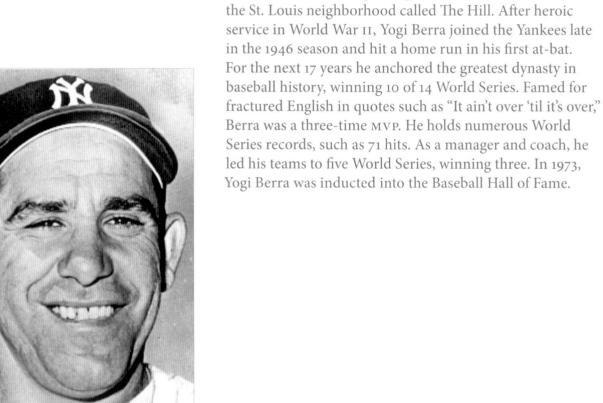

Lawrence Peter Berra grew up on Elizabeth Street in the St. Louis neighborhood called The Hill. After heroic service in World War II, Yogi Berra joined the Yankees late in the 1946 season and hit a home run in his first at-bat. For the next 17 years he anchored the greatest dynasty in baseball history, winning 10 of 14 World Series. Famed for fractured English in quotes such as "It ain't over 'til it's over," Berra was a three-time MVP. He holds numerous World Series records, such as 71 hits. As a manager and coach, he led his teams to five World Series, winning three. In 1973, Yogi Berra was inducted into the Baseball Hall of Fame.

Chuck Berry

BORN OCTOBER 18, 1926

Hailed as "The Father of Rock and Roll," Chuck Berry's signature guitar work, poetic songwriting and inspired showmanship have influenced every Rock and Roll musician to follow him. Beginning with "Maybellene" in 1955, he recorded a series of hits that defined the standards of the genre. He was the first person inducted into the Rock and Roll Hall of Fame, and is a member of the Songwriters Hall of Fame. His song "Johnny B. Goode" is on the copper records aboard the *Voyager* space probes, launched into outer space in 1977 to reach out to the universe with the best of our culture.

45

Susan Blow

BORN JUNE 7, 1843

The average poor child in 1860s St. Louis completed three years of school before being forced to begin work at age 10. Susan Elizabeth Blow addressed that problem by offering education to children earlier. Applying Friedrich Froebel's theories, she opened the United States' first successful public kindergarten at St. Louis' Des Peres School in 1873. Blow taught children in the morning and teachers in the afternoon. By 1883 every St. Louis public school had a kindergarten, making the city a model for the nation. Devoting her life to early education, Susan Blow was instrumental in establishing kindergartens throughout America.

Lou Brock

BORN JUNE 18, 1939

The greatest base stealer of his era, St. Louis Cardinal Louis Clark Brock was only the 14th player to have 3,000 hits. After three seasons with the Chicago Cubs, Brock joined the Cardinals in 1964 and fueled their World Series victory. During his 19-year career, the outfielder stole an unprecedented 938 bases and broke several World Series records, including hitting .391 in over 20 World Series games. Exemplifying the spirit of baseball on and off the field, Brock earned the Roberto Clemente and the Jackie Robinson Awards among many others. A Cardinal until he retired, Lou Brock entered the Baseball Hall of Fame on the first ballot in 1985.

Robert S. Brookings

BORN JANUARY 22, 1850

Robert S. Brookings moved from Maryland to St. Louis in 1867 to take a job as a clerk and became one of the city's most successful businessmen. In 1895 he crowned his business career with the construction of the historic Cupples Station warehouse complex in downtown St. Louis. That same year he became president of the board of Washington University, a position he held for 33 years. Brookings oversaw the university's relocation to its present location and the development of its medical school. In 1927 he founded the Brookings Institution, a leader in public policy research to this day. Robert S. Brookings devoted the latter half of his life and nearly all of his personal fortune to advance humanity through higher education.

Jack Buck

BORN AUGUST 21, 1924

John Francis Buck joined Harry Caray in 1954 to announce
St. Louis Cardinals baseball games. Their 14-year partnership
has been called the greatest broadcast team in baseball
history. Buck went on to become the anchor of the
Cardinals broadcast team and sports director of KMOX
radio. Capping each Redbird victory with a cry of "that's
a winner," Buck's wit, precision and enthusiasm earned
him CBS-TV's top play-by-play spot. Also an experienced
football commentator, he announced eight Super Bowls. In
1987 Jack Buck was inducted into Baseball's Hall of Fame.

Grace Bumbry

BORN JANUARY 4, 1937

Grace Ann Bumbry grew up at 1703 Goode Ave. in St. Louis. She joined the Union Memorial Methodist Church's choir at eleven, and sang at Sumner High School. She was a 1954 winner on *Arthur Godfrey's Talent Scouts*. After her concert debut in London in 1959, Bumbry debuted with the Paris Opera the next year. In 1961 Richard Wagner's grandson featured her in Bayreuth, Germany's Wagner Festival. The first black person to sing there, Bumbry was an international sensation and won the Wagner Medal. A mezzo-soprano who also successfully sang the soprano repertoire, Grace Bumbry recorded on four labels and sang in concerts worldwide.

William Burroughs

BORN FEBRUARY 5, 1914

Born at 4664 Pershing Ave., William Burroughs attended Community School and John Burroughs School. He was a cub reporter for the *St. Louis Post-Dispatch* in 1935. During World War II, Burroughs met Jack Kerouac and Allen Ginsberg, forming the core of "The Beat Generation." An author and visual artist, he is best-known for his writing, which is radically unconventional in technique and content. It often has been banned. His 1960 novel, *Naked Lunch*, influenced an entire generation. Burroughs was inducted into the American Academy and Institute of Arts and Letters in 1983.

Harry Caray

BORN MARCH 1, 1914

Born Harry Christopher Carabina, he grew up at
1909 LaSalle St. in St. Louis and attended Dewey School
and Webster Groves High School. He played on two local
semi-pro baseball teams before starting his radio career.
After announcing both Cardinals and Browns away
games in 1945, the effusive Caray, renowned for yelling
"Holy Cow" after big plays, broadcast for the Cardinals
from 1947 to 1969. One of baseball's best-loved announcers,
Caray then called Oakland A's and Chicago White Sox
games before capping his career with the Chicago Cubs.
In 1989 Harry Caray was inducted into the broadcasters'
wing of the Baseball Hall of Fame.

Cedric the Entertainer

BORN APRIL 24, 1964

Berkeley High graduate Cedric the Entertainer
Kyles first performed stand-up comedy at a St. Louis
open mic night. His television career began as host
of BET'S *Comic View* and as co-star of the #1-ranked sitcom
The Steve Harvey Show, for which he won four NAACP
Image Awards as Best Supporting Actor. His numerous
film performances include *The Original Kings of Comedy*,
Barbershop, *Barbershop 2*, *Be Cool*, *Johnson Family Vacation*
and *Talk to Me*. Considered one of the most prominent
comic actors of his generation, Cedric performed for two
U.S. Presidents. As a philanthropist, Cedric has given
back to the St. Louis community through his Cedric the
Entertainer Charitable Foundation.

Kate Chopin

BORN FEBRUARY 8, 1851

Katherine O'Flaherty, a member of one of St. Louis' oldest families, attended the St. Louis Academy of the Sacred Heart. When she married New Orleans native Oscar Chopin, she encountered the Creole culture which provided settings for many of her works. She wrote more than 100 short stories in the 1890s, and hosted a literary salon in her home at 3317 Morgan Street. Her 1899 novel, *The Awakening*, was condemned for its frank treatment of a young woman's sexual and artistic growth. Now it is recognized both for the quality of the writing and for its importance as an early feminist work.

Auguste Chouteau

BORN SEPTEMBER 7, 1749

Born René Auguste Chouteau in New Orleans, he was
raised by his stepfather, Pierre Laclède, and his mother,
Marie Thérèse Chouteau. As Laclède's clerk and lieutenant,
the 14-year-old Chouteau led the workers who began
building St. Louis on February 15, 1764. He prospered
as the village grew into a commercial hub, adapting to
Spanish rule in 1770 and U.S. control in 1804. Diversifying
into banking and real estate as the fur trade declined,
Chouteau, the town's business and social leader, was the
first board of trustees chairman upon its incorporation
in 1809. As an early historian of the city wrote, "Laclède
founded, and Auguste Chouteau built, St. Louis."

William Clark

BORN AUGUST 1, 1770

After the Louisiana Purchase in 1803, Thomas Jefferson asked William Clark and Meriwether Lewis to explore the newly-acquired but uncharted northwest. An Army captain, Clark set off with Lewis from St. Charles on May 14, 1804 and vividly chronicled their 28-month trek to the Pacific and back in his drawings and journal. He then lived in St. Louis until his death, serving as governor of the Missouri Territory and as Superintendent of Indian Affairs. Mourned as a great leader, his funeral procession was a mile long. The Arch stands on the spot of Lewis and Clark's return, a monument to the westward expansion pioneered by William Clark.

William "Bill" Clay

BORN APRIL 30, 1931

A native St. Louisan, William L. Clay graduated from
St. Louis University in 1953 before serving in the army.
After his election in 1959 as a St. Louis alderman, Clay
became Missouri's first African-American U.S. congressman
in 1968. During his 32 years in the House, Representative
Clay passed 295 bills and tirelessly promoted civil rights,
labor reform and education. Clay played an integral role in
the 1970 founding of the Congressional Black Caucus and
authored several books about Congress, civil rights and his
own life. A tough, savvy politician who never lost an election,
William L. Clay was a steadfast champion for human rights.

Barry Commoner

BORN MAY 28, 1917

Barry Commoner joined the faculty of Washington University in St. Louis in 1947. In 34 years there he explored viral function and led cellular research with implications for cancer diagnosis. Alarmed in the early 1950s by the health risks posed by atomic testing, Commoner helped found the St. Louis Committee for Nuclear Information. In 1966 he established the Center for the Biology of Natural Systems to study man's relationship with the environment. The author of nine books and the 1980 Citizens' Party presidential candidate, Barry Commoner, a pioneer in the creation of the environmental movement, was termed the "Paul Revere of Ecology."

Arthur Holly Compton

BORN SEPTEMBER 10, 1892

Arthur Holly Compton, a science prodigy, built and flew a glider at age 18. In 1920 he became a professor and head of the physics department at Washington University. There he deduced that x-rays, known to be waves, also act like particles. He proved it with an experiment showing the scattering action now called the Compton Effect. For that fundamental discovery, Compton won the 1927 Nobel Prize. After directing the World War II research that led to the atomic bomb, he returned to Washington University in 1945 as chancellor. In 1991 NASA named its new orbiting gamma-ray observatory after Arthur Holly Compton.

Jimmy Connors

BORN SEPTEMBER 2, 1952

A fiery left-hander known for his two-fisted backhand, Jimmy Connors grew up in East St. Louis and Belleville, Illinois. Playing tennis from the age of two, Connors thrived in St. Louis' active tennis scene and honed his amazing service return on the slick wood courts of the St. Louis Armory. He won his first pro tournament in 1972 and in 1974 he posted an astounding 99-4 match record while winning three of the four major titles. Ranked #1 in the world for over five years and in the top 10 for sixteen, Connors won 109 tournaments, including eight majors, in a career marked by versatility and tenacity. A five-time U.S. Open champion, Jimmy Connors was inducted into the International Tennis Hall of Fame in 1998.

Carl and Gerty Cori

BORN DECEMBER 5, 1896 AND AUGUST 15, 1896

Carl Ferdinand Cori and Gerty Theresa Radnitz earned
medical degrees from the German University of Prague
in 1920 and married later that year. After they joined the
Washington University School of Medicine in 1931, their
discovery of the mechanism for blood glucose regulation
earned them the Nobel Prize in 1947. Gerty Cori was
the first American woman to be so honored. In addition,
six eventual Nobel laureates received training in their
laboratory. Carl Cori said of their remarkable collaboration,
"Our efforts have been largely complementary, and one
without the other would not have gone so far…"

61

Broadcasting

Bob Costas

BORN MARCH 22, 1952

At age 22, Bob Costas joined KMOX radio in 1974 to announce St. Louis Spirits basketball games. During his seven years at KMOX, he honed the skills which fueled his career's meteoric rise. His intelligence, humor and presence led to a longtime union with NBC-TV, where he anchored the Olympics and showed his mastery of football, basketball and baseball, his first love. By age 40, Costas repeatedly had won the major sportscasting awards and proven his versatility with his acclaimed TV interview show, *Later*. Despite a demanding travel schedule, Bob Costas and his family chose to remain in St. Louis as he became a preeminent broadcast journalist.

St. Louis Walk of Fame *140 Great St. Louisans*

John Danforth

BORN SEPTEMBER 5, 1936

Already nicknamed "Senator" at Country Day High School,
St. Louisan John Danforth was elected Missouri's Attorney
General in 1968. He won a U.S. Senate seat in 1976 and
for the next 18 years unified the Senate on difficult issues,
including his landmark 1991 civil rights bill. Bipartisan
respect for his integrity led to his selection in 1999 to
investigate the federal raid at Waco and a presidential
appointment in 2001 to seek peace in the Sudan. Intent on
revitalizing St. Louis, he chaired The Danforth Foundation
and St. Louis 2004. Like his brother William, John Danforth
fully embraced his family's devotion to public service
and his hometown.

William Danforth

BORN APRIL 10, 1926

Grandson of the founder of Ralston-Purina, William Danforth took his family's deep belief in education and public service to heart. After serving as a doctor in the Navy, Danforth returned to St. Louis and joined Washington University's medical faculty in 1957. He became Chancellor of the University in 1971, an office he held for an unprecedented 24 years. Beloved by students, he united the University community and promoted academic excellence while increasing the University's endowment elevenfold. William Danforth's skillful mediation and determined leadership ensured Washington University's place as a world-class institution.

Dwight Davis

BORN JULY 5, 1879

The founder of tennis' Davis Cup, Dwight Davis was born in St. Louis. He was one of his era's best players and won several titles while at Harvard. In 1900, he founded the international competition that came to bear his name and captained the first U.S. team, which won the cup. He played in the 1904 Olympics and became St. Louis Parks Commissioner in 1911, building dozens of free tennis courts. Davis later served the game he loved as U.S. Lawn Tennis Association president, and his country as Secretary of War and Governor-General of the Philippines. The first great tennis ambassador, Dwight Davis entered the Tennis Hall of Fame in 1956.

65

Miles Davis

BORN MAY 26, 1926

The year after his birth in Alton, Illinois, Miles Davis moved to East St. Louis. He played trumpet in the jazz band at Lincoln High School and was a member of Eddie Randle's Blues Devils (a.k.a. the Rhumboogie Orchestra). By 1948 he led his own bop groups in New York. One of jazz' great bandleaders and arrangers, his milestone recordings include *Birth of the Cool*, *Kind of Blue* and *Bitches Brew*. The Encyclopedia of Jazz calls him "the most consistently innovative musician in jazz from the late 1940s through the 1960s." The Miles Davis Quintet is considered one of the outstanding groups of all time.

Dizzy Dean

BORN JANUARY 16, 1910

Known for his homespun wit and good-natured bravado,
Jay Hanna "Dizzy" Dean was perhaps the most colorful
member of the Cardinals' famed "Gas House Gang." With
his blazing fastball he won 30 games in 1934, earning MVP
honors and leading the Cardinals to a World Series victory.
He won an amazing 120 games in his first five full seasons,
but his career was cut short by injury. Dean moved on to
announce radio broadcasts of Cardinals and Browns games,
and later to television's game of the week, where his keen
analysis and informal speech charmed the nation. Dizzy
Dean was inducted into the Baseball Hall of Fame in 1953.

67

Dan Dierdorf

BORN JUNE 29, 1949

One of the greatest offensive tackles of all time, Dan Dierdorf was an All-American at the University of Michigan before joining the St. Louis Cardinals in 1971. Dierdorf and his fellow linemen anchored the Cardiac Cardinals and became one of the best lines in NFL history. They allowed the fewest sacks in the NFC for five straight seasons, and set an NFL record of only eight in 1975. Dierdorf played in six Pro Bowls and was voted the league's best blocker three times. After 13 years with the Big Red, he began a prominent broadcasting career, including more than a decade on Monday Night Football. In 1996, longtime St. Louisan Dan Dierdorf was inducted into the Pro Football Hall of Fame in his original hometown of Canton, Ohio.

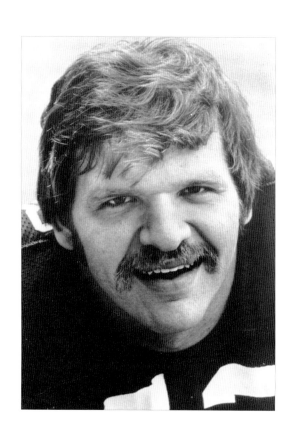

Phyllis Diller

BORN JULY 17, 1917

Born Phyllis Ada Driver, she combined wild costumes,
untamed hair and a raucous laugh with self-deprecating
monologues to create one of comedy's most popular
characters. A 1955 club booking skyrocketed her to
success: scheduled for two weeks, she stayed 89. After
moving to Webster Groves in 1961, Diller honed her act
in St. Louis clubs such as Gaslight Square's Crystal Palace.
Mid-1960s television routines featuring "Fang," her
imaginary husband, brought national acclaim. In addition
to her television, film and stage work, Phyllis Diller made
five records, wrote four best-selling books and performed
on piano with over 100 symphony orchestras.

69

Katherine Dunham

BORN JUNE 22, 1909

While studying anthropology at the University of Chicago, Katherine Dunham was also active as a dancer. Field trips to the West Indies allowed her to study native dances and folklore, which she incorporated into her work to form an exotic and unique repertoire. Following an acclaimed dance career in New York, she moved to East St. Louis in 1967, where she established the Performing Arts Training Center. The Katherine Dunham Museum and the Katherine Dunham Children's Workshop continue to expose new generations to the work of this great dancer and choreographer.

St. Louis Walk of Fame *140 Great St. Louisans*

Robert Duvall

BORN JANUARY 5, 1931

Actor Robert Duvall attended high school at
The Principia in St. Louis and graduated from nearby
Principia College in 1953. He appeared in the classic films
To Kill a Mockingbird, *True Grit* and MASH before gaining
stardom in the 1970s with unforgettable performances
in films such as *The Godfather I & II*, *Network* and
Apocalypse Now. Duvall received six Oscar nominations
in his career, and won Best Actor for 1983's *Tender Mercies*.
His television work includes *Lonesome Dove* (1989) and
Broken Trail (2006), for which he won an Emmy. A prolific
actor with unlimited range, Robert Duvall was an iconic
presence in American film for more than five decades.

James B. Eads

BORN MAY 23, 1820

The great Mississippi River bridge which bears his name is the best known of this self-educated genius' achievements. In addition, at age 22, James Eads devised the first diving bell to salvage sunken cargoes from the bottom of the river. When the Civil War began, he conceived of a fleet of armored riverboats, persuaded the Navy of its necessity, and then built the boats, which were used to capture Forts Henry and Donelson in February, 1862 – the first victories for the Union. His final engineering marvel was the system of jetties that opened the mouth of the Mississippi to seagoing ships.

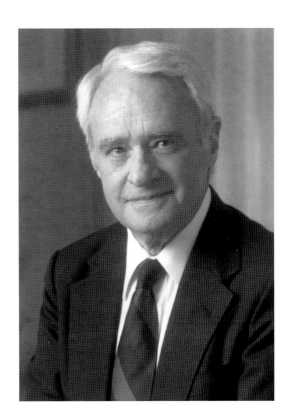

Tom Eagleton

BORN SEPTEMBER 4, 1929

Raised at 4608 Tower Grove Place, Thomas Eagleton
was only 27 when elected St. Louis Circuit Attorney.
He served as Missouri's Attorney General and Lieutenant
Governor, won a U.S. Senate seat in 1968 and sought
the Vice Presidency in 1972. He was instrumental to the
Senate's passage of the Clean Air and Water Acts, and
sponsored the Eagleton Amendment, which halted the
bombing in Cambodia and effectively ended American
involvement in the Vietnam War. After three Senate terms,
Eagleton returned to St. Louis as an attorney, political
commentator and Washington University professor.
The U.S. Courthouse in downtown St. Louis was named
for Thomas Eagleton, a devoted Missouri citizen.

Charles Eames

BORN JUNE 17, 1907

A revolutionary designer, Charles Eames was born in
St. Louis and studied architecture at Washington University.
He settled in Venice, California, where he designed some
of the most innovative furniture of the post-War modern
period with his wife Ray Kaiser. Exemplified by the Eames
Chair with its molded seat and back, Eames' furniture
combined simplicity and elegance, comfort and technology.
Over six million of the chairs were made. Often with Ray,
Eames also designed toys, buildings and fabrics, and made
almost 50 educational films. Charles Eames was elected to
the Academy and Institute of Arts and Letters in 1977.

Gerald Early

BORN APRIL 21, 1952

An inspiring educator, Gerald Early was appointed the
Merle Kling Professor of Modern Letters in English and
served as Director of Washington University's Center for
the Humanities, the American Culture Studies Program,
and the African and African American Studies Program.
The author and editor of many books and articles, he was
the winner of the 1994 National Book Critics Circle Award
for criticism and twice was nominated for Grammy Awards
for Best Album Notes. Early consulted on numerous
documentary films, most notably with Ken Burns on *Jazz*
and *Baseball*. Elected as a Fellow of the American Academy
of Arts and Sciences in 1997, in 2013 Gerald Early was
appointed by President Barack Obama to a five-year term
as a member of the National Council on the Humanities.

Buddy Ebsen

BORN APRIL 2, 1908

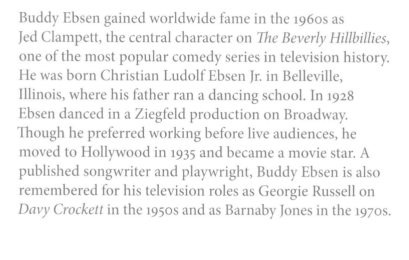

Buddy Ebsen gained worldwide fame in the 1960s as
Jed Clampett, the central character on *The Beverly Hillbillies*,
one of the most popular comedy series in television history.
He was born Christian Ludolf Ebsen Jr. in Belleville,
Illinois, where his father ran a dancing school. In 1928
Ebsen danced in a Ziegfeld production on Broadway.
Though he preferred working before live audiences, he
moved to Hollywood in 1935 and became a movie star. A
published songwriter and playwright, Buddy Ebsen is also
remembered for his television roles as Georgie Russell on
Davy Crockett in the 1950s and as Barnaby Jones in the 1970s.

T.S. Eliot

BORN SEPTEMBER 26, 1888

The grandson of the founder of Washington University, T.S. Eliot was born in St. Louis and attended Smith Academy here. He is best known as a poet and critic, and his *The Waste Land* is one of the most influential works of the twentieth century. Other noted compositions include *Portrait of a Lady*, *The Love Song of J. Alfred Prufrock*, *The Hollow Men*, *Ash Wednesday*, and *Four Quartets*. He received the Nobel Prize for Literature in 1948 and the American Medal of Freedom in 1965.

William Greenleaf Eliot

BORN AUGUST 5, 1811

Coming to St. Louis in 1834 to found a Unitarian
church, minister William Greenleaf Eliot devoted
his life to improving his adopted city. Eliot was pivotal
in developing the public school system and many other
educational and philanthropic institutions. He preached
for abolition and women's rights, and created the Western
Sanitary Commission to provide medical care and supplies
during the Civil War. His crowning achievement was the
1853 co-founding of Washington University, originally
named "Eliot Seminary." The guiding hand behind the
school's success, he served as its first president and
third chancellor. Grandfather of poet T.S. Eliot, William
Greenleaf Eliot was called "the Saint of the West"
by Ralph Waldo Emerson.

St. Louis Walk of Fame *140 Great St. Louisans*

Stanley Elkin

BORN MAY 11, 1930

Since his first novel was published in 1964, Stanley
Lawrence Elkin's literary stature has grown unabated.
A *New York Times* reviewer said, "No serious funny writer
in this country can match him." Elkin became an English
instructor at Washington University in St. Louis in 1960
and a professor in 1969. A member of the American
Academy and Institute of Arts and Letters, he received
Guggenheim and Rockefeller Foundation fellowships,
the Longview Foundation Award and the Paris Review
Humor Prize. Elkin's novella, *The Bailbondsman*, was
made into a movie. In 1982 Stanley Elkin won the
National Book Critics Circle Award.

Mary Engelbreit

BORN JUNE 5, 1952

A dedicated artist from an early age, St. Louis native
Mary Engelbreit sold her first greeting cards to a local
store while attending Visitation Academy. Inspired by
art from the 1920s and 1930s, she developed a style marked
by colorful, richly detailed drawings and short phrases
that are by turns whimsical or profound. Greeting cards
proved the perfect medium for her work, and after initial
successes, she founded her own company in 1983. By 2000
her University City headquarters oversaw a "vast empire of
cuteness" that included 12 retail stores, a national magazine
and over 6000 licensed products. Always guided by her
aesthetic vision, Mary Engelbreit's art is a gift of warmth
and joy to millions of fans.

Walker Evans

BORN NOVEMBER 3, 1903

Photographer Walker Evans was born in St. Louis
in his family home at 4468 McPherson. An artist who
sought truth and transcendence in ordinary subjects,
his most famous work documents the Depression,
including the stark portraits of Southern tenant farmers
in the book *Let Us Now Praise Famous Men*. In 1938
his *American Photographs* was the first solo exhibition
by a photographer at the Museum of Modern Art.
After 20 years in photojournalism, Evans joined the
Yale faculty in 1964. In a career that spanned five decades,
Walker Evans produced timeless images that changed
perceptions of photography and American culture.

Eugene Field

BORN SEPTEMBER 2, 1850

Eugene Field, born at 634 South Broadway in St. Louis, became a reporter for the *St. Louis Evening Journal* in 1873. Over the next decade he developed the charming and witty style that would make him America's foremost columnist. *The Chicago Morning News* hired him in 1883 to write "what I please on any subject I please." Although the resulting daily column, *Sharps and Flats*, remains a journalistic milestone, Field is remembered mainly for his children's verses. In rhymes such as "The Duel," "Little Boy Blue," and "Wynken, Blynken, and Nod," Eugene Field captured the magic and wonder of a child's imagination.

The 5th Dimension

BORN 1965

St. Louis-born singers Billy Davis Jr., LaMonte McLemore and Ron Townson joined with Marilyn McCoo and Florence LaRue to create the lush "champagne soul" sound of The 5th Dimension. The group's first top ten hits "Up, Up and Away" (1967) and "Stoned Soul Picnic" (1968) were followed in 1969 by the #1 hits "Aquarius" and "Wedding Bell Blues." Between 1967 and 1976 the group recorded over 20 Top 40 singles, won six Grammy Awards and produced two network television specials. A musical source of hope, joy and sincerity during tumultuous times, The 5th Dimension were described by Frank Sinatra as "without a doubt the freshest, most musical, most capable group in today's bag."

Curt Flood

BORN JANUARY 18, 1938

Proclaimed "Baseball's Best Centerfielder" on a 1968 *Sports Illustrated* cover, three-time All-Star Curtis Charles Flood played 12 seasons for the St. Louis Cardinals. Flood won seven straight gold gloves from 1963 through 1969, hit .293 for his career and helped the Cardinals win the 1964 and 1967 World Series. Flood sued Major League Baseball when he was traded in 1969, asserting, "I do not feel I am a piece of property to be bought and sold irrespective of my wishes." The legal battle effectively ended his playing career. The U.S. Supreme Court ruled against his suit in 1972, but Curt Flood's stand helped the players win free agency in 1975, and passage of the Curt Flood Act in 1998 limited baseball's antitrust exemption.

Redd Foxx

BORN DECEMBER 9, 1922

Redd Foxx starred in *Sanford and Son*, one of television's most popular comedy series in the 1970s. Born John Elroy Sanford in St. Louis, he left home at age 16 to join a New York street band. Called Red for his complexion, he adopted a baseball star's name to become Redd Foxx. Honing his comic skills in the 1940s, he became one of the nation's funniest nightclub comics, although his racy language limited his exposure. His 50 off-color "party" records reached a larger audience, selling more than 20,000,000 copies. A dramatic role in the 1970 film *Cotton Comes to Harlem* paved the way to television stardom for Redd Foxx.

David Francis

BORN OCTOBER 1, 1850

David Rowland Francis came to St. Louis in 1866 and graduated from Washington University in 1870. A successful businessman, he was elected mayor of St. Louis in 1885 and governor of Missouri in 1888; he later served as Secretary of the Interior from 1896 through 1897 and was U.S. Ambassador to Russia during the 1917 Russian Revolution. As president of the Louisiana Purchase Exposition, Francis made the 1904 St. Louis World's Fair a globally celebrated event. David Francis simultaneously attracted the 3rd modern Olympiad to St. Louis, and the 1904 Olympic venues Francis Gymnasium and Francis Field are still in use on Washington University's campus.

Joe Garagiola

BORN FEBRUARY 12, 1926

Joseph Henry Garagiola grew up on Elizabeth Street in the St. Louis neighborhood called The Hill. Signed at 16 by Branch Rickey, Garagiola played for the Cardinals in five seasons, including the 1946 championship year. After his pro career ended in 1954, he joined St. Louis radio station KMOX and broadcast Cardinals games the next year. After moving to the Yankees, Garagiola called baseball for NBC for 27 years. Two stints with *The Today Show* capped his illustrious broadcast career. A 1973 winner of television's Peabody Award, Joe Garagiola entered the broadcasters' wing of the Baseball Hall of Fame in 1991.

Dave Garroway

BORN JULY 13, 1913

Moving to St. Louis at age 14, David Garroway attended University City High School and Washington University. After training as a radio announcer while an NBC page in New York, he worked in Pittsburgh and then Chicago, where he returned after serving in World War II. His popular jazz radio show led to *Garroway at Large*, perhaps the most innovative early television variety show. Recognizing the appeal of his unconventional and relaxed manner, NBC chose him in 1952 as the first host of *Today*, the original national morning show. Transatlantic telecasts and an on-air chimpanzee exemplified the originality of David Garroway, the man who helped wake up a nation.

William Gass

BORN JULY 30, 1924

A consummate author with a philosopher's training, William Gass joined the Washington University faculty in 1969 and received an endowed chair in 1979. Gass introduced audiences to his polished, energetic prose with the 1966 novel *Omensetter's Luck* and the classic book of short stories *In the Heart of the Heart of the Country*. Two essay collections earned National Book Critics Circle Awards for Criticism, and in 1995 Gass completed his monumental novel *The Tunnel*. A distinguished artist deeply concerned with the issues writers face, William Gass was named director of the International Writers Center in 1990.

Literature

Martha Gellhorn

BORN NOVEMBER 8, 1908

Martha Gellhorn grew up at 4366 McPherson in
St. Louis and graduated from John Burroughs in 1926.
A gifted writer of novels and short stories – *In Sickness
and in Health* won the 1958 O. Henry Award – Gellhorn's
honest prose and reckless daring made journalism her
best work. She covered the Spanish Civil War, stowed away
on a hospital ship to land at Normandy on D-Day, and
in 1966 reported from Vietnam on the war. Her acerbic
memoir *Travels with Myself and Another* (1978) tells of her
"best horror journeys," many with her estranged second
husband Ernest Hemingway. At once glamorous, witty
and courageous, Martha Gellhorn was eulogized as "the
premier war correspondent of the 20th century."

St. Louis Walk of Fame *140 Great St. Louisans*

Bob Gibson

BORN NOVEMBER 9, 1935

Robert Gibson, once a Harlem Globetrotter, pitched for
the St. Louis Cardinals from 1959 until he retired in 1975.
Known for his fastball, he struck out 3,117 batters. In his
1968 MVP season, Bob Gibson pitched 28 complete games
and 13 shutouts while setting a National League record
with a 1.12 ERA Pitching in three World Series, Gibson was
the MVP of the Cardinals' two championships. His Series
records include seven consecutive complete–game wins
and 17 strikeouts in one game. Winner of nine Gold Gloves
and two Cy Young Awards, he was also a feared hitter. In
1981 Bob Gibson was inducted into the Baseball Hall of Fame.

John Goodman

BORN JUNE 20, 1952

A native son of Affton in St. Louis County, John Goodman studied drama at Southwest Missouri State and later made his mark with distinctive, often hilarious character performances in films such as *True Stories* and *Raising Arizona*. Drawing on his St. Louis roots for inspiration, Goodman starred from 1988 through 1997 as Dan, the lovable, working-class husband on the acclaimed television series *Roseanne*. Also a talented stage actor, Goodman moved to leading roles in films such as *The Babe* and *The Flintstones*. Admired by his peers and immensely popular with his fans, John Goodman's work reveals a gifted, down-to-earth actor with tremendous range.

Betty Grable

BORN DECEMBER 18, 1916

Betty Grable was born at 3858 Lafayette Ave. in St. Louis
and moved to the Forest Park Hotel in 1920. She entered
Clark's Dancing School at age 3 and attended Mary
Institute. When only 12 she went to Hollywood and got her
first film role the next year. She acted in 42 films, including
Tin Pan Alley, *Moon Over Miami* and *Coney Island*. Because
of her world-renowned swimsuit poster, owned by one
out of every five U.S. servicemen in World War II, her legs
were insured for $1,000,000. Betty Grable was Hollywood's
top draw in 1943, and was reported to be the richest
woman in the United States.

Evarts Graham

BORN MARCH 19, 1883

One of the 20th century's most prominent surgeons, Evarts A. Graham chaired the Department of Surgery at Washington University from 1919 to 1951. Under his direction, it became a world leader in surgical procedures and training. Graham performed the world's first successful removal of an entire lung at Barnes Hospital in 1933; his 49 year-old patient lived another 30 years. Graham pioneered techniques to detect gallbladder disease and engaged in momentous research linking cigarette smoking to lung cancer. An advocate for ethical medical practices, Evarts A. Graham's "influence radiated over every aspect of the national and international surgical scene."

Ulysses S. Grant

BORN APRIL 27, 1822

Upon graduating from West Point in 1843, U.S. Grant
was assigned to Jefferson Barracks, near St. Louis. There
he married Julia Dent, whose family estate, White Haven,
was nearby. He left the army in 1854 to work his wife's farm,
which he called "Hard Scrabble." He left after four years to
open a real-estate agency in St. Louis. Appointed brigadier
general by President Lincoln early in the Civil War, Grant
captured Forts Donelson and Henry in February 1862.
After further successes he was named commander of the
Union army, which he led to victory. He became the 18th
president of the United States in 1869.

Dick Gregory

BORN OCTOBER 12, 1932

Born in St. Louis, Dick Gregory grew up at 1803 N. Taylor Ave. shining shoes to help feed his family. At Sumner High School, he led a march against conditions in segregated schools and set a state record in track. As a star comedian in the early 1960s, he used biting racial satire and shunned the stereotypes of early black comics. Prompted by Martin Luther King, Jr., he became a civil rights and anti-war leader, running for president in 1968 and fasting for human rights both here and abroad. Bringing wit and dedication to countless causes for decades, Dick Gregory started the "Campaign for Human Dignity" in 1992 to fight crime in St. Louis neighborhoods.

Charles Guggenheim

BORN MARCH 31, 1924

Documentary filmmaker Charles Guggenheim started his
first production company in St. Louis in 1954. A four-time
Oscar winner, he received his first of 12 Academy Award
nominations in 1956 for *A City Decides*, a film about the
integration of St. Louis public schools. A pioneer in the
field of campaign films, Guggenheim also made two
feature films, most notably 1959's *The Great St. Louis Bank
Robbery*, starring a then unknown Steve McQueen. His
1968 masterpiece *Monument to the Dream* documented
construction of the St. Louis Arch. Still shown daily on the
Arch grounds, Charles Guggenheim said it was one film on
which he would not change a single frame.

Robert Guillaume

BORN NOVEMBER 30, 1927

An actor who defied racial stereotypes, Robert Guillaume grew up in downtown St. Louis and studied music at Washington University. After building a successful stage and musical career, in 1977 he assumed his trademark role as television's Benson. Guillaume insisted that the wisecracking butler "be African-American and be equal;" the character later became lieutenant governor, while Guillaume won Emmys in 1979 and 1985. He earned rave reviews as the lead in *Phantom of the Opera* in 1990 and won a Grammy for his reading of *The Lion King*. Robert Guillaume's career proves that race need not define the role and talent can overcome prejudice.

John Hartford

BORN DECEMBER 30, 1937

Growing up in University City and attending John
Burroughs School, John Hartford was drawn to river life
and the music of the banjo and fiddle. He earned two
Grammys in 1967 for "Gentle on My Mind," one of the
most recorded and broadcast songs ever. Always original
yet faithful to tradition, Hartford crafted over 30 albums,
including the 1976 Grammy-winner *Mark Twang*. Famous
for his unique one-man show, at times he performed on a
riverboat after piloting it the same day. A gifted musician,
author and folk music historian, John Hartford became a
powerful voice for his twin muses, the river and its music.

Donny Hathaway

BORN OCTOBER 1, 1945

Soul singer Donny Hathaway grew up in St. Louis and graduated from Vashon High in 1963. Already an accomplished producer, composer and musician, in 1970 he released the album *Everything Is Everything*, which included the R&B hit "The Ghetto." Hathaway released two outstanding studio albums in the next three years, as well as *Donny Hathaway Live* and an album of duets, *Roberta Flack & Donny Hathaway*. He collaborated frequently with Flack, and the duo earned two Top 10 hits: 1972's Grammy-winning "Where Is the Love" and 1978's "The Closer I Get to You." Admired by generations of fans and fellow musicians, Donny Hathaway's influence on soul, R&B and pop music far outweighed his relatively brief recording career.

Whitey Herzog

BORN NOVEMBER 9, 1931

Beloved Cardinal manager Dorrel "Whitey" Herzog
enjoyed a solid eight-year playing career from 1956 to
1963, but in his own words, "Baseball has been good to me
since I quit trying to play it." He managed the Kansas City
Royals to three straight division titles from 1976 to 1978
and was hired as Cardinal manager in 1980. His brand
of "Whiteyball," based on speed, defense and pitching,
electrified Cardinal fans for 10 seasons. Herzog won three
pennants and the 1982 World Series title with the Cardinals,
and was named National League manager of the year in
1985. Finishing his managerial career with 1,281 wins and a
.532 winning percentage, Whitey Herzog was inducted into
the Baseball Hall of Fame in 2010.

Al Hirschfeld

BORN JUNE 21, 1903

Albert Hirschfeld was born in a house on Kensington Avenue in St. Louis. His family moved to New York when he was 12 and by age 18 he was artistic director at Selznick Pictures. After the *New York Times* printed one of his theater sketches in 1927, Hirschfeld emerged as a master of the line drawing. For over six decades he captured the essence of the theater's personalities with a few pen strokes. Often drawn in a dark theater, Hirschfeld's works became intrinsic to Broadway culture. Assessing their stature, one critic wrote, "There are just two forms of fame on Broadway: seeing your name in lights, and more significantly, to be drawn by Hirschfeld."

William Holden

BORN APRIL 17, 1918

Actor William Holden was born near St. Louis in O'Fallon,
Illinois. He vaulted to stardom in 1939's *Golden Boy*, and
the film's title stuck as Holden's nickname. He received
the first of three Academy Award nominations for 1950's
Sunset Boulevard, then won Best Actor for 1953's *Stalag 17*.
A versatile leading man, Holden starred in classics such as
Sabrina (1954), *Picnic* (1955), *The Bridge on the River Kwai*
(1957) and *The Wild Bunch* (1969). He received his final
Oscar nomination for *Network* (1976) and won an Emmy
for the television film *The Blue Knight* (1973). One of the
greatest movie stars of the 20th century, William Holden
was named to the AFI's list of Hollywood's 50 greatest
screen legends.

Rogers Hornsby

BORN APRIL 27, 1896

Baseball's greatest right-handed hitter, Rogers Hornsby was the cornerstone of the Cardinals' first winning era. He won a total of seven batting titles, including his 1924 century-best mark of .424. Also a powerful hitter, he led the league in slugging nine times and home runs twice. He managed the Cardinals to their first championship in 1926 while still a full-time player. Hornsby lived in St. Louis even after being traded and was player-manager for the St. Louis Browns from 1933 to 1937. A two-time league MVP and 1942 Hall of Fame inductee, Rogers Hornsby compiled a National League record .358 career average.

A.E. Hotchner

BORN JUNE 28, 1920

Born in St. Louis, Aaron Edward Hotchner grew up
in the Westgate Hotel at Delmar and Kingshighway,
and attended Soldan High School. A 1941 Washington
University Law School graduate, he served as a military
journalist before becoming a successful editor, novelist,
playwright and biographer. Respected for giving all profits
from a joint venture with actor Paul Newman to charities
and the arts, Hotchner is best known for *Papa Hemingway*,
his biography of close friend Ernest Hemingway. *King of
the Hill*, A.E. Hotchner's evocative novel about growing
up in St. Louis during the Great Depression, was captured
on film in 1993.

105

William Inge

BORN MAY 3, 1913

Born in Independence, Kansas, William Inge taught at Stephens College before coming to St. Louis as the *Star-Times* drama critic in 1943. Encouraged and inspired by Tennessee Williams, Inge finished his first play in 1947. While teaching at Washington University from 1946 through 1949, he wrote the award-winning *Come Back, Little Sheba*. Like *Bus Stop* (1955) and the Pulitzer Prize-winning *Picnic* (1953), it earned acclaim on Broadway and in Hollywood. His screenplay *Splendor in the Grass* won an Academy Award in 1962. The dominant playwright of the 1950s, William Inge captured the essence of Midwestern life.

Hale Irwin

BORN JUNE 3, 1945

After winning the 1967 NCAA golf championship, Hale Irwin turned pro in 1968 and later settled in St. Louis. His first PGA tour victory came in 1971, and in 1974 he won the first of his three U.S. Open Championships. A self-taught player, Irwin was known for discipline, precision shot-making and intense competitiveness. Irwin scored 20 victories on the PGA Tour and was elected to the World Golf Hall of Fame in 1992. In 1995 he joined the Champions Tour, where he achieved a record 45 wins. His annual pro-am tournament raised millions to benefit St. Louis Children's Hospital, and in 1995 the hospital dedicated the Hale Irwin Center for Pediatric Hematology/Oncology in his honor.

107

William B. Ittner

BORN SEPTEMBER 4, 1864

Unhappy with the prison–like schools of his youth,
St. Louis-born architect William B. Ittner devoted his
life to improving education through better school design.
Appointed St. Louis School Board commissioner in 1897,
he designed open buildings that featured natural lighting,
inviting exteriors, and classrooms tailored to specific needs.
His 50 St. Louis schools include Wyman Elementary (1901)
and Sumner High (1908). Ittner's other works include the
Scottish Rite Cathedral (1921) and the Continental Building
(1929), a crowning example of St. Louis Art Deco. William
B. Ittner designed over 500 schools nationwide and has
over 35 buildings on the National Register of Historic Places.

Johnnie Johnson

BORN JULY 8, 1924

Self–taught pianist Johnnie Johnson settled in St. Louis in 1952 and formed the Sir John Trio. He asked Chuck Berry to sit in that New Year's Eve, and a magical, half-century collaboration was born. Johnson provided the driving undercurrent on many Berry classics. His inspired piano playing in the 1987 film *Hail! Hail! Rock & Roll* earned him a new generation of fans, including Keith Richards and Eric Clapton, both of whom played on his album *Johnnie B. Bad*. Other albums and international tours followed. Always a loyal sideman, Johnnie Johnson emerged as a star in his own right.

Scott Joplin

BORN NOVEMBER 24, 1868

In the 1880s and 90s, as ragtime music evolved from
the African rhythms of its creators' heritage, its greatest
composer, Scott Joplin, was often in St. Louis, playing
piano in the bawdy houses and saloons of Market and
Chestnut streets. He moved to Sedalia, Missouri in 1896
to work at The Maple Leaf Club, which gave its name to
one of his most popular rags. Returning to St. Louis in
1901, Joplin lived at 2658-A Morgan (later re-named
Delmar Blvd.) His more than 50 published works
include *The Entertainer* and *The Cascades*, inspired by
the waterfalls of the 1904 Worlds Fair. In 1976 a special
Pulitzer Prize was awarded for his opera, *Treemonisha*.

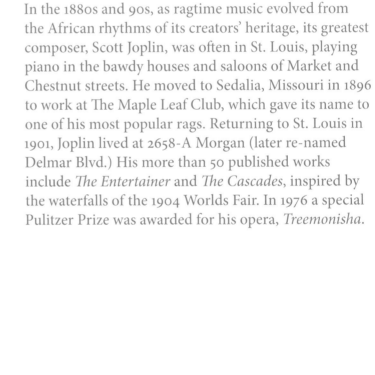

Jackie Joyner-Kersee

BORN MARCH 3, 1962

The greatest female athlete of the 20th century, Jackie Joyner-Kersee grew up in East St. Louis and was a two-sport All-American at Lincoln High. She won six Olympic medals, including two golds and a silver in the grueling heptathlon. Battling asthma and injury throughout her career, she won her last long jump medal in 1996 with a heroic final leap. She moved back to the St. Louis metro area and in 2000 opened her most prized accomplishment – a youth center bearing her name – in East St. Louis. An inspiration to women around the world, Jackie Joyner-Kersee's incomparable excellence and dedication elevated the stature of women's sport.

Albert King

BORN APRIL 25, 1923

Born Albert Nelson, he was a farm laborer who became a premier blues guitarist. Self-taught, first on a one-string "diddley-bow" and then on a guitar he made from a cigar box, King played left-handed and upside down. In 1956 he moved to Lovejoy, Illinois, across the river from St. Louis. King perfected his searing guitar sound in the historic 1950s and 60s St. Louis blues and R&B scene. In 1966 he signed with the Stax label, where he recorded such classics as "Crosscut Saw" and "Born Under A Bad Sign." After a legendary 1968 Fillmore West concert series and recording, Albert King was called "the most-imitated blues guitarist in the world."

Kevin Kline

BORN OCTOBER 24, 1947

A St. Louis native and Priory School graduate, Kevin Kline won Tony Awards for *On the Twentieth Century* and *The Pirates of Penzance* before leading roles in *Sophie's Choice* (1982) and *The Big Chill* (1983) made him a Hollywood star. Adept at comedy and drama on stage and screen, Kline won an Academy Award for his madcap performance in *A Fish Called Wanda* and received accolades for his stage interpretations of *Richard III* and *Hamlet*. Refusing to abandon his passion for theater while working in films as diverse as *Dave* and *Cry Freedom,* Kevin Kline often has been called the "American Olivier."

113

Pierre Laclède

BORN NOVEMBER 22, 1729

French-born Pierre Laclède Liguest arrived in New Orleans in 1755. He ventured up the Mississippi in 1763 to build a trading post after his firm won trading rights in the upper Louisiana Territory. Choosing a site near the mouth of the Missouri, he sent his stepson, Auguste Chouteau, to start the settlement in February 1764. Naming it St. Louis, Laclède laid out streets, made property assignments and governed until territorial officials arrived in October 1765. Laclède, who brought his library to the wild, owned the town's first industry, a water-powered mill. St. Louis' first citizen, Pierre Laclède envisioned his village becoming "one of the finest cities in America."

St. Louis Walk of Fame *140 Great St. Louisans*

Rocco Landesman

BORN JULY 20, 1947

Broadway producer Rocco Landesman was born and
raised in St. Louis, where his family owned the Crystal
Palace, a Gaslight Square cabaret that featured cutting
edge theater and performers. Landesman developed and
produced the Broadway musical *Big River*, which won
seven Tony Awards in 1985. He was named president
of Jujamcyn Theaters in 1987, where he emphasized the
development of new plays and produced significant
works such as the Tony-winners *Angels in America* and
The Producers. A larger than life figure who has owned
racehorses and baseball teams as well as theaters, in 2009
Rocco Landesman was named chairman of the National
Endowment for the Arts.

Aviation

Charles A. Lindbergh

BORN FEBRUARY 4, 1902

One of the finest fliers of his time, Charles Lindbergh was the chief pilot for the first St. Louis-to-Chicago airmail route, in April 1926. While based at Lambert Field, he conceived of an airplane that could fly from New York to Paris, and persuaded a group of St. Louis businessmen to finance the project. The result was the immortal *Spirit of St. Louis*, which he flew across the Atlantic on May 20–21, 1927. The feat made Lindbergh a national hero and raised public awareness of aviation's potential to an unprecedented level.

Theodore Link

BORN MARCH 17, 1850

One of the city's greatest architects, German-born
Theodore Link came to St. Louis in 1873. He designed
over 100 buildings, including his home at 5900 West
Cabanne Place, mansions at 29 and 38 Portland Place
and Grace Methodist Church on Skinker Blvd. He also
designed the Mississippi State Capitol and Louisiana State
University. Link's crowning achievement was St. Louis'
Union Station. Completed in 1894, it was the largest station
of its time and is considered an architectural "jewel." The
first to use electric light decoratively and a leader of the
Romanesque Revival movement, Theodore Link left
St. Louis a grand and enduring legacy.

Elijah Lovejoy

BORN NOVEMBER 9, 1802

Elijah Parish Lovejoy, a Presbyterian minister and editor of the *St. Louis Observer*, believed that slavery was a sin. First calling for gradual emancipation, he later became an abolitionist, but in the violent climate of 1830s St. Louis, neither stand was tolerated by slavery's proponents. Although threatened, Lovejoy insisted on the public's right to "hear both sides and let the right triumph." Seeking safety, he moved to Alton, Illinois, but mobs there smashed three printing presses. Defending a fourth *Observer* press in 1837, Lovejoy was murdered, shocking the nation. In giving his life for freedom of the press, Elijah Lovejoy gave us a better knowledge of its value.

Ed Macauley

BORN MARCH 22, 1928

A loyal native whose mother allowed him to choose any
college that was "Catholic and in St. Louis," Ed Macauley
led the Saint Louis University basketball team to the 1948
NIT national championship and won AP player of the year
in 1949. Later a high-scoring Boston Celtics star, "Easy Ed"
made All-NBA three straight years and was MVP of the
first All-Star game in 1951. He won an NBA title with the
St. Louis Hawks in 1958 and then coached them to the
finals in 1960. Active in St. Louis charities throughout his
life, Macauley was ordained a Catholic Deacon in 1989 and
co-authored the book *Homilies Alive*. Inducted into the
Basketball Hall of Fame in 1960, Ed Macauley was named
one of the game's 100 greatest players in 1990.

Marsha Mason

BORN APRIL 3, 1942

Born in St. Louis, Marsha Mason began acting at Nerinx Hall High and Webster College. After nearly a decade on and off-Broadway, she catapulted to film stardom with *Cinderella Liberty* (1973), for which she received an Academy Award Nomination and won the first of her two Golden Globe Awards. From 1977 through 1981 she earned Oscar nominations for *The Goodbye Girl*, *Chapter Two* and *Only When I Laugh*, all written by her then-husband Neil Simon. While still appearing in films, Mason later returned her focus to the theater. She also was nominated for an Emmy in 1997 for her work on television's *Frasier*. Lauded for her portrayals of contemporary women, Marsha Mason became a leading actress of her generation.

Masters
and Johnson

BORN DECEMBER 27, 1915
& FEBRUARY 11, 1925

William Howell Masters began researching sexual function
at the Washington University School of Medicine in 1954.
Virginia Eshelman Johnson joined him three years later.
Their investigation of the physical aspects of sexuality
produced some of the first reliable data in the field.
Human Sexual Response, Masters and Johnson's first book,
was published for the medical community but became a
best seller. They opened the Masters and Johnson Institute
in 1964 to provide sex therapy and counseling based on
their findings. The research, books and media activities of
Masters and Johnson profoundly affected American society.

121

Bill Mauldin

BORN OCTOBER 29, 1921

William Henry Mauldin joined the Army newsletter *Stars and Stripes* as a cartoonist during World War II. There he perfected Joe and Willie, the muddy, weary "dogfaces" who portrayed the drabness of the foot soldier's life. Despised by the conservative brass as disrespectful but loved by G.I.s as their own, the cartoons won Bill Mauldin a 1945 Pulitzer Prize. A self-styled "stirrer-upper," Mauldin joined the *St. Louis Post-Dispatch* in 1958. Dubbed "the hottest editorial brush in the U.S.," he won his second Pulitzer Prize that year. Syndicated in over 250 newspapers, Bill Mauldin battled injustice and pretense with irony and humor.

Virginia Mayo

BORN NOVEMBER 30, 1920

Noted for her striking beauty, Virginia Mayo was one of the most successful actresses of the 1940s and 1950s. Born Virginia Jones in St. Louis, she began training at her aunt's drama school at age six. She graduated from Soldan High School and danced for the Muny Opera before Samuel Goldwyn signed her to a Hollywood contract. Mayo made almost 50 movies, including *White Heat*, *She's Working Her Way Through College* and *The Best Years of Our Lives* and appeared in 20 stage productions and many TV shows. Called "tangible proof of God's existence" by the Sultan of Morocco, Virginia Mayo received one of the original stars on Hollywood Boulevard.

Michael McDonald

BORN FEBRUARY 12, 1952

Born and raised in the Ferguson area of St. Louis, Michael McDonald attended McCluer High School and performed locally with The Majestics and Jerry Jay and The Sheratons before moving to Los Angeles in 1970. After two years with Steely Dan, McDonald joined the Doobie Brothers in 1975, writing and singing hits such as "Takin' It to the Streets," "Real Love" and the #1 "What a Fool Believes." Going solo in 1982, McDonald had a top ten hit with "I Keep Forgettin' (Every Time You're Near)" and reached #1 again on his 1986 duet with Patti Labelle, "On My Own." A five-time Grammy winner, Michael McDonald helped define the blue-eyed soul sound of the 1970s and 1980s.

Robert
McFerrin Sr.

BORN MARCH 19, 1921

Baritone Robert McFerrin moved to St. Louis in 1936
and began classical voice training at Sumner High. He
sang on Broadway and with the National Negro Opera
Company, and in 1955 became the Metropolitan Opera's
first African-American male soloist. McFerrin provided
the vocals for Sidney Poitier in the 1959 film classic
Porgy and Bess and toured and taught internationally
before returning to St. Louis in 1973. A severe stroke in
1989 impaired his verbal ability but not his voice, and he
courageously resumed performances, including concerts
with his Grammy-winning son, Bobby. In 2003 Opera
America honored Robert McFerrin Sr. with a lifetime
achievement award.

125

David Merrick

BORN NOVEMBER 27, 1911

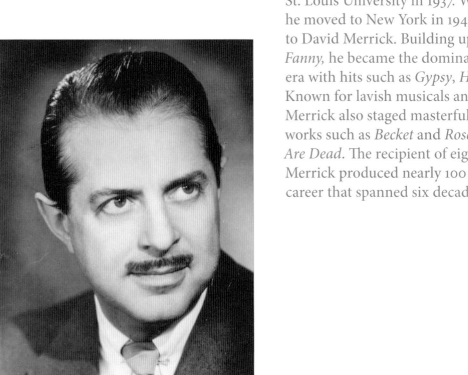

Born and raised in St. Louis, David Margulois graduated from Central High in 1930 and received a law degree from St. Louis University in 1937. With his sights on Broadway, he moved to New York in 1940 and changed his name to David Merrick. Building upon the success of 1954's *Fanny,* he became the dominant Broadway producer of his era with hits such as *Gypsy, Hello, Dolly!* and *42nd Street.* Known for lavish musicals and outlandish publicity stunts, Merrick also staged masterful productions of imported works such as *Becket* and *Rosencrantz and Guildenstern Are Dead.* The recipient of eight Tony Awards, David Merrick produced nearly 100 Broadway shows in a career that spanned six decades.

Archie Moore

BORN DECEMBER 13, 1913

Born Archibald Lee Wright, Hall of Fame boxer
Archie Moore was raised in St. Louis. Moore began
his professional career fighting locally in 1936, but his
impressive record and imposing knockout style caused
champions to avoid him. Moore finally got a title shot in
1952 at the age of 39, winning the light heavyweight crown
before a hometown crowd in St. Louis. He held the belt for
nine years, and nearly defeated Rocky Marciano for the
heavyweight title in 1955. Nicknamed "The Old Mongoose,"
he notched a record 131 knockouts over a 27-year career. As
generous outside the ring as he was unrelenting inside it,
Archie Moore devoted himself to serving underprivileged
children throughout his life.

127

Marianne Moore

BORN NOVEMBER 15, 1887

Born in Kirkwood, poet Marianne Moore was profoundly influenced by her early upbringing in the St. Louis area before her family moved to Pennsylvania. One of the most influential early modernists and an inspiration to generations of women poets, Moore is known for her keen sense of detail and her precise use of language. She published many volumes of acclaimed poetry in 50 years, including *Collected Works* (1951), which won a Pulitzer Prize and a National Book Award. Also an essayist and translator, Moore was modest and skeptical of her own writing, but others saw her genius. T.S. Eliot said the work of Marianne Moore is "part of the small body of durable poetry."

Agnes Moorehead

BORN DECEMBER 6, 1900

Agnes Moorehead moved to St. Louis as a child, where she acted in stage productions, danced with the Muny Opera and debuted as a radio singer on KMOX in 1923. After moving to New York and appearing on Broadway, she became a charter member of Orson Welles' famous Mercury Theater, starring in hundreds of radio dramas. Following her 1941 movie debut in *Citizen Kane*, she displayed her range as a character actress in over 60 films and also played Endora on TV's *Bewitched* from 1964 to 1972. One of the best acting voices in radio history, Agnes Moorehead also received four nominations for Academy Awards.

Stan Musial

BORN NOVEMBER 21, 1920

Stan Musial was one of the greatest players in the history of baseball. A gentleman both on the field and off, "Stan the Man" played his entire 22 year professional career with the St. Louis Cardinals. He had a lifetime .331 batting average, with 3,630 base hits and 475 home runs and held numerous records when he retired. Musial won seven league batting titles and three Most Valuable Player awards, and he helped the Cardinals win three world championships. He was inducted into the Baseball Hall of Fame in 1969.

Nelly

BORN NOVEMBER 2, 1974

Born Cornell Haynes Jr., Nelly formed the St. Lunatics
in 1993 with friends from University City High. His 2000
solo debut *Country Grammar* topped the Billboard charts,
sold over 9 million copies and put St. Louis hip-hop in
the national spotlight. 2002's multi-platinum *Nellyville*
included the #1 single "Hot in Herre," which earned
Nelly one of his three Grammy Awards. Nelly reached
new audiences by acting in the films *Snipes* (2001) and
The Longest Yard (2005), and reached out to the public
by founding the charity 4Sho4Kids. Throughout Nelly's
considerable artistic evolution, his music always found
its soul in his hometown of St. Louis.

Howard Nemerov

BORN MARCH 1, 1920

Howard Nemerov graduated from Harvard in 1941,
served in World War II and began teaching in 1946.
His first volume of poetry, *The Image and the Law*, was
published the next year. In 1969, he became professor
of English at Washington University. In addition to 13
volumes of poetry, his works include novels, stories and
a notable body of criticism. He was inducted into the
American Academy and Institute of Arts and Letters in
1977. *The Collected Poems of Howard Nemerov* won the
National Book Award and the Pulitzer Prize a year later.
He was named Poet Laureate of the United States in 1988.

Gyo Obata

BORN FEBRUARY 28, 1923

Gyo Obata, a Washington University graduate, co-founded the St. Louis architecture firm Hellmuth, Obata & Kassabaum in 1955. It attained global prominence, largely due to Obata's designs. His influence on the St. Louis skyline is profound. The Priory Chapel, Boatmen's Tower, Cervantes Convention Center & Stadium, Forsythe Plaza, Metropolitan Square, One Bell Center, the Children's Zoo and Living World and the Union Station renovation are but a few of Obata's St. Louis projects. The National Air and Space Museum, the airport and university in Riyadh, Saudi Arabia, and the Taipei World Trade Center exemplify the worldwide work of Gyo Obata.

Marlin Perkins

BORN MARCH 28, 1902

Marlin Perkins came to the St. Louis Zoo in 1926 to
work with the reptile collection. He became curator of
the Buffalo Zoo in 1938. As director of Chicago's Lincoln
Park Zoo in 1949, he created the Peabody Award-winning
television show *Zoo Parade*. In 1962 Perkins returned to
the St. Louis Zoo as director. He debuted *Wild Kingdom* in
1963, hosting it until 1985. Winner of four Emmy Awards, it
taught a generation about animals in their habitats and is
in the Television Hall of Fame. The American Association
of Zoological Parks & Aquariums' top honor for achievement
has been named the Marlin Perkins Award.

Mike Peters

BORN OCTOBER 9, 1943

One of America's preeminent cartoonists, Mike Peters was born and raised in St. Louis. After graduating from CBC High, he earned a fine arts degree at Washington University in 1965. By 1972 his editorial cartoons were syndicated nationally; in 1981 they won him a Pulitzer Prize. In 1984 he launched the zany, enormously popular comic strip *Mother Goose & Grimm*, eventually published in more than 800 newspapers worldwide. The recipient of virtually every major honor in his profession, Peters has published over 40 collections of his work. Imbued with both a charming, boyish sense of humor and a satirist's ready wit, the cartoons of Mike Peters are equally at home on the comic and editorial pages.

Bob Pettit

BORN DECEMBER 12, 1932

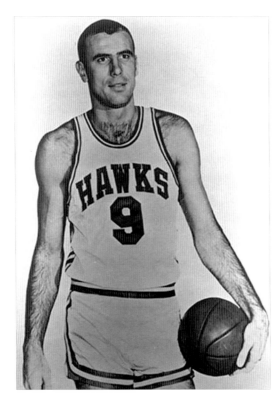

Basketball legend Bob Pettit came to St. Louis with the Hawks in 1955. The ideal power forward, he averaged 26.4 points and 16.2 rebounds per game for his career. Pettit led the Hawks to the NBA Finals four times in five years, and in the 1958 Finals he scored 50 points in the deciding Game 6 to clinch the team's only championship. Pettit was named MVP of the NBA All-Star Game an astonishing four times and made the team in each of his 11 seasons. He retired in 1965 as the first NBA player to score 20,000 points. A 1971 inductee into the Basketball Hall of Fame, two-time league MVP Bob Pettit was named one of the 50 greatest players in NBA history.

Vincent Price

BORN MAY 27, 1911

Called "The King of Horror," Vincent Price is best
known for his villainous roles in more than 100 films,
as well as many stage and television productions, but his
accomplishments cover a much broader range. He is a
connoisseur of fine art and the author of a number of
books on the subject. A collector as well, he bought
a Rembrandt drawing at age 12 while still living in the
family house on Forsyth Blvd. Price, who is also the
author of several gourmet cookbooks, graduated from
Community School and St. Louis Country Day School.

Joseph Pulitzer

BORN APRIL 10, 1847

A native of Hungary, Joseph Pulitzer emigrated to
the U.S. in 1864 and served in the Union Army during
the Civil War. He moved to St. Louis in 1868 to work
as a reporter for a German-language newspaper. He
bought the bankrupt *St. Louis Dispatch* in 1878 and soon
merged it with the *Evening Post* to form the *St. Louis
Post-Dispatch*. Pulitzer, an exponent of high journalistic
standards, endowed the Columbia School of Journalism.
His greatest legacy is his annual award for excellence in
journalism – the Pulitzer Prize.

Harold Ramis

BORN NOVEMBER 21, 1944

A Chicago native, Harold Ramis attended Washington University in St. Louis and graduated in 1966. Inspired by life in a fraternity house on Forsyth Boulevard, Ramis co-wrote the 1978 collegiate farce *Animal House*, the first of his box-office hits. In the 1980s he wrote and starred in *Stripes* and *Ghostbusters* and directed *Caddyshack* and *National Lampoon's Vacation*. In 1993 he wrote and directed the mature comedy *Groundhog Day* and later directed 1999's *Analyze This* and 2002's *Analyze That*. A dedicated Washington University alumnus and member of its board, Harold Ramis deftly combined wry wit and slapstick into some of Hollywood's most popular and beloved comedies.

139

Judy Rankin

FEBRUARY 18, 1945

St. Louis-born golf prodigy Judy Torluemke began playing at age six and honed her skills at the "Triple A" golf course in Forest Park. Described as one of the best prospects ever in a 1961 *Sports Illustrated* cover article, she turned pro in 1962 and won her first tour event in 1968. The first LPGA player to top $100,000 in winnings for a season, she was named LPGA Player of the Year in 1976 and 1977. After retiring in 1983 with 26 tour victories, Rankin became a top television commentator for women's and men's events and captained the U.S. team to consecutive Solheim Cup victories in 1996 and 1998. Recipient of golf's Patty Berg, Bob Jones and Ben Hogan Awards, Judy Rankin was inducted into the World Golf Hall of Fame in 2000.

Peter Raven

BORN JUNE 13, 1936

Born in China, Peter Raven was a professor at Stanford
University before moving to St. Louis in 1971 to head the
Missouri Botanical Garden. Under his direction, it became
the leading tropical plant research facility in the world,
its staff racing to catalog species doomed to extinction.
Raven stressed that the destruction of each rainforest is
"one more step toward creating a world in which we cannot
live." A preeminent scientist and professor at Washington
University, Peter Raven became a world-renowned
champion of the environment, lecturing around the
globe and writing dozens of books and articles to
stop man's decimation of life-giving plants.

Paul C. Reinert, S.J.

BORN AUGUST 12, 1910

A dominant force in Saint Louis University's rise in national stature, Father Paul C. Reinert, S.J. earned three degrees there before joining the faculty in 1944. He was the university's president from 1949 to 1974 and chancellor from 1974 to 1990. Believing education should be accessible to all, he worked tirelessly to revitalize both the university and the surrounding midtown community. A recognized leader in education, Reinert served many national organizations and wrote two significant books on higher education. Recipient of nearly 40 honorary doctorates and countless awards for his service, Paul C. Reinert was foremost a "Jesuit and a priest," selfless in his pursuit of educational reform.

Branch Rickey

BORN DECEMBER 20, 1881

Often called the greatest front-office strategist in baseball
history, Branch Rickey came to the Cardinals in 1917 and
turned a losing team into a powerhouse. Believing that
"luck is the residue of design," he developed the modern
farm system that brought the Cardinals nine pennants
and six World Series through the 1940s. After moving to
the Brooklyn Dodgers, Rickey signed Jackie Robinson and
brought him to the majors in 1947; more black players soon
followed. Branch Rickey simultaneously broke baseball's
color line and built the great Dodger teams of the 1940s and
1950s, ensuring his induction into the Baseball Hall of Fame.

143

The Rockettes

BORN 1925

In 1925 Russell Markert formed the "Missouri Rockets," a 16-member dance line that performed before feature films at the Missouri Theater on Grand Avenue. Seven years later the group's performance at the opening night of Radio City Music Hall led to a permanent engagement and a name change to the Rockettes. Known for their eye-high kicks, uniformly glamorous appearance and the absolute precision of their routines, onstage the 36 Rockettes appear to move as one dancer. An icon of Americana, the Rockettes' performances have included the 1937 Paris Exposition, the USO in World War II, the 1988 Super Bowl and the 2001 Presidential inauguration.

Irma Rombauer

BORN OCTOBER 30, 1877

Already known as one of the city's most charming hostesses, St. Louis native Irma Rombauer risked her own funds to publish *The Joy of Cooking* in 1931. As the Depression forced more American families to cook for themselves, Rombauer's wit and common sense made the chore more pleasurable, and her engaging tone put amateurs at ease. With the 1943 edition, it became the nation's most popular cookbook; later revisions, including those by her heirs, continue to meet changing tastes. Comprehensible, comprehensive and fun, Irma Rombauer's *The Joy of Cooking* became a fixture in America's kitchens.

Charles M. Russell

BORN MARCH 19, 1864

Charles Marion Russell's more than 3,000 paintings, drawings and sculptures captured the essence of the American West. Born in St. Louis, he grew up at Oak Hill, his family's country estate near present-day Tower Grove Park. Russell, who moved to Montana at age 15 to be a cowboy, was a professional artist by 1893. Within a decade he was nationally-recognized for the accuracy with which he rendered his subjects. Russell was also an able storyteller whom Will Rogers called the best he ever heard. One of the premier artists of the American West, Charles M. Russell lovingly preserved the rugged splendor of the frontier.

David Sanborn

BORN JULY 30, 1945

Saxophonist David Sanborn grew up in Kirkwood and began playing in St. Louis area clubs as a teen. He backed legends like Albert King, Little Milton and Gil Evans, then joined the Paul Butterfield Blues Band in 1967, later playing with them at Woodstock. For decades he worked with music's biggest names, from Miles Davis and James Brown to the Eagles and the Rolling Stones. 1975's *Taking Off* launched a solo career that in the 1980s produced five Grammys in jazz, R&B and pop; Sanborn added a sixth Grammy for 1999's *Inside*. Whether on his own works like *Voyeur*, collaborations such as *Double Vision* or hundreds of recordings with other artists, David Sanborn left an indelible mark on the music of his time.

Red Schoendienst

BORN FEBRUARY 2, 1923

Albert "Red" Schoendienst joined the Cardinals in 1945, his first of over 50 consecutive years in a big league uniform. The Cardinals' second baseman for over a decade, his spectacular defense and solid hitting helped them capture the 1946 World Series. Selected to ten all-star teams, he captained the star-studded Milwaukee Braves to two World Series before rejoining the Redbirds. Schoendienst managed the Cardinals for a team-record 12 years, winning the 1967 World Series, and coached for many more. A 1989 Hall of Fame inductee, Red Schoendienst was only the sixth Cardinal player to have his number retired.

Dred and Harriet Scott

BORN CIRCA 1799 AND CIRCA 1820

Remembered for the infamous 1857 decision that denied them their freedom, Dred and Harriet Scott spent much of their adult lives enslaved in St. Louis. In the 1830s, Dred Scott's slave owner took him to the free state of Illinois and then to federal territory, where slavery was prohibited. While there, he married Harriet. They were returned to St. Louis in 1838, and in 1846 began a courageous 11-year legal battle for emancipation based on their time spent in free territory. The U.S. Supreme Court's decision withheld the fundamental rights of citizenship from Dred and Harriet Scott – and all black Americans – propelling the nation toward civil war.

149

Ntozake Shange

BORN OCTOBER 18, 1948

Born Paulette Williams, writer Ntozake Shange lived in St. Louis from 8 to 13 years of age on Windemere Place in The Ville. Her experiences in St. Louis infuse her work, especially the novels *Betsey Brown* (1985) and *Liliane: Resurrection of the Daughter* (1994). She won an Obie award for her electrifying stage play *For Colored Girls Who Have Considered Suicide/When the Rainbow is Enuf.* Now a standard of the American stage, the 1976–77 Broadway hit was adapted into a major motion picture in 2010. A prodigious author of poetry collections, novels and essays as well as plays, Ntozake Shange's work combines technical innovation and lyric exuberance with a passionate feminist voice writing from an African-American perspective.

Henry Shaw

BORN JULY 24, 1800

Henry Shaw, only 18 when he came to St. Louis, was
one of the city's largest landowners by age 40. Working
with leading botanists, he planned, funded and built the
Missouri Botanical Garden, which opened in 1859. Shaw
donated the land for Tower Grove Park and helped with
its construction. He wrote botanical tracts, endowed
Washington University's School of Botany, helped found
the Missouri Historical Society and gave the city a school
and land for a hospital. Of Shaw's gifts, the Botanical
Garden is best-known. Said as early as 1868 to have
"no equal in the United States, and, indeed, few anywhere
in the world," it epitomizes the legacy of Henry Shaw.

William T. Sherman

BORN FEBRUARY 8, 1820

One of the greatest Civil War generals, William T. Sherman first settled his family in St. Louis in 1851. The West Point graduate captured Atlanta in 1864 and then led the "March to the Sea," a scorched-earth campaign designed to end the South's ability to wage war. Given command of the entire Army in 1869, Sherman moved his headquarters to St. Louis five years later. Retiring from the army in 1884, Sherman repeatedly was offered the nomination for president but declined. A celebrated commander who warned that war "is all hell," William T. Sherman was buried in St. Louis' Calvary Cemetery in 1891.

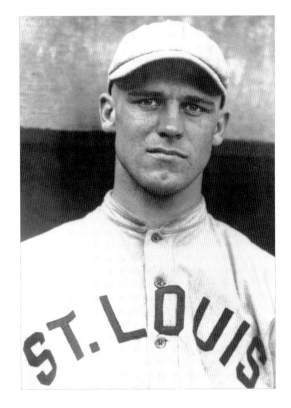

George Sisler

BORN MARCH 24, 1893

The greatest player in St. Louis Browns history, "Gentleman" George Sisler was arguably baseball's most complete first baseman. Intelligent and athletic, he won two batting titles, led the league in steals four times and was one of the finest fielders ever. In 1920 he batted .407 and his 257 hits set a record that stood until 2004. League MVP in 1922, "The Sizzler" hit .420 and heroically led the mediocre Browns to within a game of the pennant. He finished his career with a .340 average and lived the rest of his life in St. Louis. Elected to the Hall of Fame in 1939, George Sisler was described by Ty Cobb as "the nearest thing to a perfect ballplayer."

153

Leonard Slatkin

BORN SEPTEMBER 1, 1944

Leonard Slatkin studied violin, viola and piano as a child and made his Carnegie Hall conducting debut at age 22. The leading American conductor of his generation, he was named music director of the Saint Louis Symphony Orchestra in 1979. He has earned critical praise for his work there and with ensembles around the globe. Slatkin and the symphony have received wide acclaim, including numerous Grammy nominations and awards. Lauded for his commitment to American music, adventurous programming and superb performances and recordings, Leonard Slatkin has emerged as one of the world's great conductors.

Jackie Smith

BORN FEBRUARY 23, 1940

With his rare combination of size, speed and competitive intensity, Jackie Smith redefined the position of tight end in the NFL. The St. Louis Cardinals drafted the Louisiana track and football star in 1962, and he became a fixture with the Big Red for 15 seasons. Timed at 9.8 seconds in the 100-yard dash, Smith's speed made him a unique offensive threat among tight ends, and hard work turned him into a punishing blocker. He played in five consecutive Pro Bowls, and was named All-Pro in 1967 when he caught 56 passes for 1,205 yards and 9 touchdowns. The leading receiver among tight ends when he retired, Jackie Smith was elected to the Pro Football Hall of Fame in 1994.

155

Ozzie Smith

BORN DECEMBER 26, 1954

The greatest defensive shortstop of all time, Osborne Earl "Ozzie" Smith anchored the thrilling "Runnin' Redbirds" teams that appeared in three World Series, winning in 1982. A spectacularly acrobatic yet rock-steady fielder, "The Wizard's" eye-popping defensive gems made him a fan favorite and earned him 13 consecutive Gold Gloves. The 15-time All-Star steadily improved his offense after joining the Cardinals in 1982 and ended his 19-year career in 1996 with 2,460 hits, 1,257 runs and 580 stolen bases. A fixture in the St. Louis community and one of the most popular Cardinal players ever, Ozzie Smith was elected to the Baseball Hall of Fame on the first ballot in 2002.

Willie Mae Ford Smith

BORN JUNE 23, 1904

The music we now call gospel was thought too worldly in 1917 when Willie Mae Ford moved to St. Louis, but she was to change that. Rather than deny the power of the blues, she enfolded it in her religious convictions to form a joyous new message of praise. Having helped found the National Convention of Gospel Choirs and Choruses, she organized its Soloists' Bureau in 1939. Profoundly influencing almost every gospel singer to follow, she was featured in the 1983 film *Say Amen, Somebody*. Willie Mae Ford Smith received the Heritage Award from the National Endowment for the Arts In 1988.

157

Max Starkloff

BORN SEPTEMBER 18, 1937

Disabled in an auto accident in 1959, lifelong St. Louisan Max Starkloff never surrendered to dependence or inaction. In 1970 he co-founded Paraquad, a pioneering Center for Independent Living, and in 2003 he co-founded the Starkloff Disability Institute. His advocacy secured legislation for public improvements like curb cuts, disabled parking and the passage of the landmark Americans with Disabilities Act in 1990. Co-founder of the National Council on Independent Living in 1983 and winner of the President's Distinguished Service Award in 1991, Max Starkloff's grass roots activism and expertise on disability issues improved the lives of millions of Americans.

Sara Teasdale

BORN AUGUST 8, 1884

Sara Teasdale was born in St. Louis and lived both on Lindell Blvd. and on Kingsbury Place. While attending Mary Institute and Hosmer Hall, she began writing poems. First published in 1907, Teasdale wrote several collections of poetry in the following decade and became known for the intensity of her lyrics. In 1918 *Love Songs* won what was essentially the first Pulitzer Prize for Poetry. Expressing disenchantment with marriage, Teasdale's later poetry resonated with suffering and strength. According to one biographer, Sara Teasdale spoke for "women emerging from the humility of subservience into the pride of achievement."

Clark Terry

BORN DECEMBER 14, 1920

Born in St. Louis, Clark Terry made his first trumpet out of garden hose, attended Vashon High School and played in local clubs before joining a Navy band during World War II. His years with Count Basie and Duke Ellington in the late 1940s and 1950s established him as a world-class jazz artist. Blending the St. Louis tone of his youth with contemporary styles, Terry's sound influenced a generation, including Miles Davis. Also a pioneer of the fluegelhorn in jazz, Terry was a standout in the NBC-TV Orchestra for 12 years before he left to form his own bands and continue recording. Clark Terry was inducted into the National Endowment for the Arts Jazz Hall of Fame in 1991.

Kay Thompson

BORN NOVEMBER 9, 1909

Known as Kitty Fink at Soldan High and Washington University, St. Louis-born Kay Thompson began her career as a singer in Hollywood. At MGM she wrote and arranged songs for films like *The Ziegfeld Follies* and *The Harvey Girls* in 1946. Thompson also won acclaim for her unique nightclub performances and her role in 1957's *Funny Face*. In 1955 she published *Eloise*, a book about a mischievous six-year-old living in New York's Plaza Hotel. Loved by children and "precocious grown-ups," *Eloise* and three sequels sold one million copies by 1963. *Eloise Takes a Bawth*, published posthumously in 2002, introduced Kay Thompson's alter ego to a new generation of readers.

Henry Townsend

BORN OCTOBER 27, 1909

A great blues guitarist and pianist, Henry Townsend grew up near Cairo, Illinois. After moving to St. Louis, he made his first record in 1929. During the 1930s, he played with many of the early blues giants, including Walter Davis, Roosevelt Sykes and Robert Johnson. The author of hundreds of songs and sideman on countless recordings, Townsend became the patriarch of St. Louis blues, was featured in a BBC documentary and recorded in each of eight decades. Recognized as a "master artist," he received the National Heritage Award in 1985. *Blues Unlimited* magazine called Henry Townsend "a commanding genius of a musician."

Helen Traubel

BORN JUNE 16, 1899

Born above her father's drugstore at Jefferson and
Chouteau Avenues in south St. Louis, heroic-voiced
Helen Traubel debuted with the St. Louis Symphony in
1924. To continue her training in St. Louis, she initially
declined an offer from New York's Metropolitan Opera,
but moved to New York in the late 1930s. Traubel was the
Met's premier Wagnerian soprano until she left in 1953 to
appear in nightclubs, on television and in movies. With
her joyous confidence and booming laughter, Helen
Traubel broke down barriers in a stratified society
and proved that an American could succeed in the
European-dominated opera world.

Ernest Trova

BORN FEBRUARY 19, 1927

Ernest Tino Trova, a self-trained St. Louis native, became one of the most significant artists of the late twentieth century. Best known for his signature image, the *Falling Man*, Trova considered his entire output a single "work in progress." A collector of classic American comic character toys, Trova admired their surrealism and used them in some of his pieces. He began as a painter, progressing through three-dimensional constructions to his mature medium, sculpture. Trova's gift of 40 of his works led to the opening of the Laumeier Sculpture Park. With his *Falling Man*, Ernest Trova created one of the defining artistic images of his time.

Ike Turner

BORN NOVEMBER 5, 1931

Ike Turner played a profound role in shaping American
music. His band's 1951 single "Rocket 88" is often regarded
as the first Rock and Roll record. As a talent scout and
A&R man, he discovered or recorded many blues legends,
including Elmore James, Buddy Guy and Howlin' Wolf.
Turner moved to East St. Louis in 1954, and his Kings of
Rhythm became a top rhythm & blues act in St. Louis.
In the 1960s the group's sound evolved into the pulsating
Rock and Roll of Ike & Tina Turner. Famous for his boogie-
woogie piano and whammy-bar guitar signatures, Turner
produced hits such as "A Fool in Love," "It's Gonna Work
Out Fine" and "Proud Mary." Ike Turner was inducted into
the Rock and Roll Hall of Fame in 1991.

165

Tina Turner

BORN NOVEMBER 26, 1939

Her powerful voice and the raw intensity of her stage shows brought Tina Turner rhythm & blues fame in the 1960s. Born Anna Mae Bullock in Nutbush, Tennessee, she moved to St. Louis at age 16. She was a student at Sumner High School when she joined Ike Turner and the Kings of Rhythm. With the 1960 hit "A Fool in Love," they became the Ike & Tina Turner Revue. In 1977 Tina left to pursue a solo career that took her to the top of the Pop, Rock and R&B charts. She won three 1984 Grammy Awards, including Record of the Year for *What's Love Got to Do With It*. In 1991 Tina Turner was inducted into the Rock and Roll Hall of Fame.

Mona Van Duyn

BORN MAY 9, 1921

In 1947 Mona Van Duyn co-founded *Perspective: A Quarterly of Literature* with her husband, Jarvis Thurston. Moving to St. Louis in 1950, they published it for another 30 years. Van Duyn's first book of poetry, *Valentines to the Wide World*, was published in 1959. One of the nation's preeminent poets, she won the Bollingen Prize, the National Book Award, the Academy of American Poets fellowship and the Ruth Lilly Award. Van Duyn, whose poetry finds large truths in small subjects, won the 1991 Pulitzer Prize for poetry for her seventh book, *Near Changes*. In 1992 Mona Van Duyn was named Poet Laureate of the United States.

Dick Weber

BORN DECEMBER 23, 1929

Among the greatest bowlers in history and a leading ambassador for the sport, Dick Weber became a St. Louisan in 1955 when he joined the legendary Budweiser bowling team. A charter member of the Professional Bowlers Association, Weber won bowler of the year in 1961, 1963 and 1965. With amazing longevity and consistency, he won 4 All-Star titles, 11 All-American Team honors, 26 PBA tournaments and 6 senior titles in an unprecedented five decades, and was inducted into both major bowling halls of fame. Dick Weber's textbook form, consummate skill and devotion to his sport epitomized class on and off the lanes.

Mary Wickes

BORN JUNE 13, 1910

Born and raised in St. Louis, comedic actress
Mary Wickes graduated from Beaumont High and
Washington University. Her big break came in the 1939
Broadway hit *The Man Who Came to Dinner*; Wickes
reprised her role in the 1941 film version. Famous for
playing sharp-tongued busybodies, nurses, nuns and
do-gooders, Wickes appeared in over 50 films, ranging
from classics like *White Christmas* and *The Music Man* to
the 1992 hit *Sister Act*. An accomplished television actress,
veteran of 27 major Broadway productions, and member
of the St. Louis Muny Hall of Fame, Mary Wickes
delighted audiences for an incredible seven decades.

Tennessee Williams

BORN MARCH 26, 1911

One of the greatest twentieth-century playwrights, Tennessee Williams attended Soldan and University City high schools, and Washington University, before graduating from the University of Iowa. His plays explore what he called "the unlighted sides" of human nature with great insight. He won Pulitzer Prizes for *Streetcar Named Desire* and *Cat on a Hot Tin Roof*. Those works, along with *Glass Menagerie* and *Night of the Iguana*, also won New York Drama Critics Circle Awards. Williams wrote nearly thirty full-length plays, two novels, and a number of short stories and plays.

Shelley Winters

BORN AUGUST 18, 1920

Born Shirley Schrift in an apartment on Newstead Ave. in St. Louis, she was in the Veiled Prophet pageant at age four. She left high school to become a model, studying acting at night. A gifted performer who fought Hollywood's stereotypes, Shelley Winters earned an Oscar nomination for the 1945 film *Double Life*, her first major role. Devoted to Method acting, she appeared in 50 plays as well as more than 100 films and television shows. A frequent award nominee, she received a 1964 Emmy for *Two Is the Number*. Shelley Winters won two Academy Awards, for *The Diary of Anne Frank* in 1959 and *A Patch of Blue* in 1965.

Harriett Woods

BORN JUNE 2, 1927

Dedicated to women's participation at all levels of government, Harriett Woods began her political career on the University City Council in 1967 and became the first woman elected statewide in Missouri in 1984. As a state senator and as Lieutenant Governor, she led reforms to aid society's most vulnerable: the elderly, minorities, the homeless. As president of the National Women's Political Caucus from 1991 to 1995, Woods helped a record number of women win elections and achieve senior White House appointments. Combining vision and political skill, Harriett Woods engendered a new level of respect for women in politics.

Chic Young

BORN JANUARY 9, 1901

Cartoonist Murat Bernard "Chic" Young grew up in
St. Louis at 2148 Oregon Ave. and graduated from
McKinley High in 1919. In 1930 Young created *Blondie*,
a comic strip featuring Blondie Boopadoop and her
boyfriend Dagwood Bumstead. Readership jumped after
the couple married in 1933, eventually reaching 250 million
as the Bumstead family merrily depicted the joys and
tribulations of middle class life. *Blondie* inspired radio,
film and television series and introduced the world to the
"Dagwood" sandwich. Chic Young produced over 15,000
Blondie installments by the time of his death in 1973, after
which the strip was created by his son Dean and flourished
into the 21st century.

Acknowledgements

Project Director Joe Edwards

Editing Brad Hines, Hope Edwards, Tom Peckham, Joe Edwards

Book Design Hope Edwards

Photographs of Induction Ceremonies
Hope Edwards, Jennifer Silverberg, Linda Edwards

Production Assistant Teresa Kitchens

Ceremony Music St. Louis River Critters Band

Inductee Portrait Photo Credits to Institutions

Missouri History Museum, St. Louis
Josephine Baker, Susan Blow, Kate Chopin, Auguste
Chouteau, William Clark, Carl and Gerty Cori, T.S. Eliot,
Eugene Field, Ulysses S. Grant, Pierre Laclède, Theodore
Link, Charles M. Russell, Willie Mae Ford Smith,
Sara Teasdale, Helen Traubel

The St. Louis Mercantile Library Association
Henry Armstrong, Yogi Berra, Lou Brock, Harry Caray,
Dizzy Dean, Dan Dierdorf, Katherine Dunham,
James B. Eads, Charles Eames, William Greenleaf Eliot,
Redd Foxx, Dave Garroway, Bob Gibson, Betty Grable,
Al Hirschfeld, Rogers Hornsby, William Inge, Charles
Lindbergh, Marsha Mason, Bill Mauldin, David Merrick,
Archie Moore, Marianne Moore, Agnes Moorehead,
Stan Musial, Vincent Price, Harold Ramis, Branch
Rickey, Irma Rombauer, Red Schoendienst, Dred and
Harriet Scott, William T. Sherman, Clark Terry,
Kay Thompson, Tina Turner, Mary Wickes,
Tennessee Williams

Washington University/Herb Weitman
Arthur Holly Compton, Howard Nemerov,
Mona Van Duyn

Individual Photographers/Photographic Contributors

Josephine Baker: Richard Martin

Jack Buck: Larry Sherron

Stanley Elkin: Joan Elkin

Mary Engelbreit: Rich Saal

Walker Evans: Metropolitan Museum of Art 1994.256.391
Paul Grotz (American, b. Germany, 1902-1990),
Walker Evans, 1930-34 ©The Metropolitan Museum
of Art, Walker Evans Archive, 1994

Charles Guggenheim: Berko Studio

Donny Hathaway: Gilles Pétard Collection

Johnnie Johnson: Joe Frisch

Scott Joplin: Scott Joplin State Historic Site

Albert King: Wart Enterprizes/David Horwitz©

Rocco Landesman: Michael Eastman

Elijah Lovejoy: Elijah Parish Lovejoy Society

Masters & Johnson: photograph by Buzz Taylor

Nelly: Universal Records ©2004

Gyo Obata: H.O.K.

Mike Peters: Greg Preston

Joseph Pulitzer: *St. Louis Post-Dispatch*; portrait by
John Singer Sargent, photographed by D. Gulick

Judy Rankin: David Cannon/Getty Images

Charles M. Russell: Pollard

David Sanborn: Henry Leutwyler

Henry Shaw: Portrait Collection, Missouri Botanical
Garden Library; painting by Fairchild & Rox

George Sisler: National Baseball Library, Cooperstown, NY;
courtesy St. Louis Cardinals Hall of Fame Museum

Jackie Smith: NFL Photos, Prolook/Image, photographed
by Herb Weitman

Willie Mae Ford Smith: Jackie Jackson

Henry Townsend: Bill Greensmith Photography

Community Support

We invite you to become a supporting member of this non-profit 501(c)(3) project that brings pride, knowledge and inspiration to St. Louisans year after year.

Patrons who donate a cumulative $250 or more will have their names added to the following list of supporters in future editions of this book, be listed on the website and receive other benefits as well as gratitude.

special support from

Private Contributors

Anonymous
Bill and Mary Abkemeier
Tom Aldridge
Chuck Berry
Anne and Dick Bischoff
Mark and Ramsey Botterman
Joan Bray and Carl Hoagland
Ed Brimer
Steve Broderson
Bill Bueler, Jr.
Jessica Bueler
Madelene Campbell
Mr. and Mrs. Bud Carlson Jr.
Captain Bill Carroll
Jeff Clinton
Jerry Clinton
Jeff and Rebecca Cook
Ken and Kathleen Cook
Jim Damos
Roberta Dearing
Jim Deatherage
Joe and Nancy deBettencourt
Mary and Wallace Diboll

Christine Edwards
Hope Edwards
Joe Edwards
Linda Edwards
Ed Finkelstein
Sister Margaret Finnie, S.L.
John Forrester
Margaret Garner
Marvin and Sandra Ginsberg
Lil Goldman
Mark Gorman
Mary Gorman
Salim Hanna
Ray Hartmann
Stan Hoffman
Claudia Horn
Shawn Jacobs
Rose Jonas
Dee Joyner
Mr. Ralph Kalish and
      Ms. Eleanor Withers
Phil and Randa Klasskin
Robert J. Krehbiel

Dr. William Landau
Arthur Lieber, Jr.
Ms. Mary Lieber
Larry and Joy Lieberman
Bob and Judy Little
Dennis Lutsky
John D. Mandelker
Dave Mastin
Alan McClain
Fran Sontag McNeal
Ted and Emilie Meiners
Eric Mink
Ralph Morse
Jeff Mugg
Talmage and Sara Newton
Won Park
Carol Perkins
Mr. and Mrs. Thomas J. Purcell, Jr.
Leon and Ann Robison
Larry and Carol Rossel
David Rothschild
Pete and Donna Rothschild
Eleanor Ruder

Private Contributors, cont.

Jenny and Mark Sadow
Steve Schankman
Rick Schaumberger
Sondra and Milton Schlesinger
Paul and Suzanne Schoomer
Ken and Mary Schuman
Dr. and Mrs. Edward H. Schwarz
Mary Ann and Mike Shanahan
Mary Ann Shaw
Dr. and Mrs. Eli and Renni Shuter
Gentry Smith
Judy and Ernest Stix

Sidney L. Stone
Steven M. Stone
Bob and Barb Suberi
Greg Sullivan
Mr. and Mrs. Andrew C. Taylor
Dan Tierney
John Thompson
Doug and Sheri Tollefsen
Dave and Alanna Trauterman
J. Kim Tucci
Norma Vavra and Wallace Klein
Nancy and Bob Wagner

Dan and Robin Wald
Lana Wald
Margaret Wald, in memory of
Sam Wald
Sandy Wald
Dave and Corinne Walentik
Don Walker
David S. Weiss
Allan Welge
Mrs. Ben Wells
Gerald and Sandy Wool
Simon Yu

Commercial/Foundation Contributors

A. Brooks Co.
AdVentures Screenprinting
ARCO Construction Co.
Backstage Galleries
Big Shark Bicycle Co.
Blueberry Hill
Carl Safe Design Consultants
Cicero's
Colonial Carpet Co.
Commerce Bancshares Foundation
Commerce Bank of University City
Componere Gallery
Coolaire Company
Craft Alliance Gallery
Eclipse Restaurant
Emerson
Emerson Charitable Trust
Engraphix
Fitz's

G.A. Sullivan
The Gatesworth
GlaxoSmithKline Foundation
Grey Eagle Distributors
Hochschild, Bloom & Company LLP
H.S.B. Tobacconist
Jeffrey M. Clinton Memorial
    Foundation
Loop Automotive
Loop Subway
Mary Engelbreit Studios
The Melting Pot
Missouri Ornamental Iron
Northwest Refrigeration
Parkview Gardens Association
Peacock Loop Diner
Photographic Resources
Plowsharing Crafts
Pulitzer Publishing Co. Foundation

Regional Arts Commission
St. Louis Design Alliance
St. Louis Smoothie
Saint Louis University
Saleem's Restaurant
Shell/Chris Kemph
Signature Beer Co.
Smoothie King
Square
Stone & Alter Real Estate Co.
Streetside Records
The Loop Special Business Districts
Tivoli Theatre
Vintage Vinyl
Washington University in St. Louis
William T. Kemper Foundation
Wonder Novelty

Special thanks to former University City Mayors Janet Majerus and
Joe Adams, Mayor Shelley Welsch, members of the University City
Council, St. Louis City Mayor Francis Slay, Alderwoman Lyda Krewson
and the citizens of University City and the City of St. Louis for providing
the sidewalks of The Loop as the location for the St. Louis Walk of Fame.

This book is dedicated to the people of St. Louis, who have provided the
cultivating cultural environment for people to fully realize their talents
and bright ideas and to powerfully contribute to our national heritage.